Harry Teel's No Nonsense

Guide To Fly Fishing
Central & Southeastern Oregon

Learn About Fly Fishing 40 of Oregon's Finest Rivers, Streams, Lakes and Reservoirs

- The Best Water
- The Best Flies To Use
- The Best Time to Fish
- How To Get There
- Equipment You'll Need
- Accommodations & Services

Acknowledgements

The author thanks the following people for their assistance and comments during this guides production: my wife Dee, who toiled for hours on the home computer. Joanne Dunac, Bill Nelson and Jeff Perin for their review of the text. David Banks for his constructive input on all elements of this guide. Their contributions were of immeasurable value.

Copyright © 1993 by
David Marketing Communications.

Published and distributed by
David Marketing Communications
6171 Tollgate, Sisters, Oregon 97759 U.S.A.

Printed by Maverick Publications, Inc.
No part of this book may be reproduced, stored in a retrievable system, or transmitted in any form, or by any means, electronic, mechanical, photocopying or otherwise, without the prior permission of the publishers. Printed in Bend, Oregon

ISBN: 0-9637256-0-2

Editor: David Banks
Maps: Harry Teel
Cover Photo: Brad Teel
Covers: Peter Speach, David Banks

*T*his guide is dedicated to my wife, Delores, and my five children, Brad, Bruce, Susan, Brett and Shelley, who, under duress at times, accompanied me on numerous fishing excursions and. . . .

To my many fishing friends who have taught me the fine points of reading water, casting, selecting flies, the necessity of good equipment and how to camp in perfect misery on a beautiful, warm summer day.

VICINITY MAP

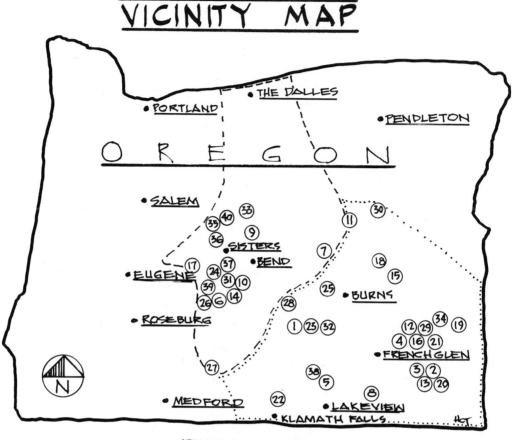

REFERENCED
STREAMS, LAKES and RESERVOIRS

1 ANA RIVER
2 ANKLE CREEK
3 BIG and LITTLE INDIAN CREEKS
4 BLITZEN RIVER
5 CHEWAUCAN RIVER
6 CRESCENT CREEK
7 CROOKED RIVER
8 DEEP CREEK
9 DESCHUTES RIVER
10 FALL RIVER
11 JOHN DAY RIVER
12 KIGER CREEK
13 LITTLE BLITZEN RIVER
14 LITTLE DESCHUTES RIVER
15 MALHEUR RIVER
16 McCOY CREEK
17 McKENZIE RIVER
18 NORTH FORK, MALHEUR RIVER
19 OWYHEE RIVER
20 SKULL CREEK

21 WILDHORSE CREEK
22 WILLIAMSON RIVER
23 ANA RESERVOIR
24 CRANE PRAIRIE RESERVOIR
25 CHICKAHOMINY RESERVOIR
26 DAVIS LAKE
27 DIAMOND LAKE
28 DUNCAN RESERVOIR
29 FISH LAKE
30 GRINDSTONE RANCH LAKES
31 HOSMER LAKE
32 LAKE OF THE DUNES
33 LAKE BILLY CHINOOK
34 MANN LAKE
35 ROUND LAKE
36 SUTTLE LAKE
37 THREE CREEKS LAKE
38 THOMPSON RESERVOIR
39 WICKIUP RESERVOIR
40 METOLIUS RIVER

Table of Contents

Section I

Section II

* *The McKenzie River and Diamond Lake are really
not in the Central Oregon zone, but since so many
people from the region fish these waters, and since
they're right on our "border," Harry Teel has
taken the liberty to include them.*

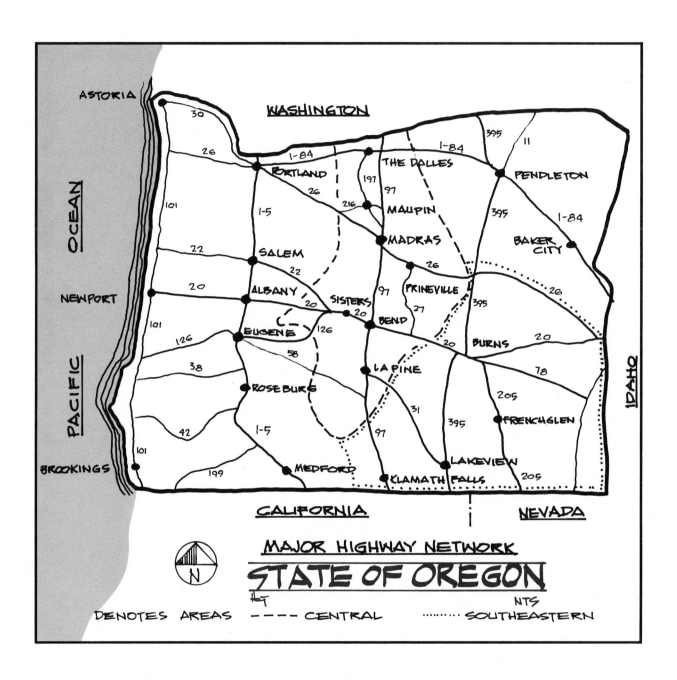

Preface

I'm very fortunate in many ways. But as this fortune relates to fly fishing, I'm fortunate that I was born in Oregon, and fortunate that I was introduced to fly fishing by my father and his friends at a very early age. These circumstances have allowed me to pursue trout, steelhead and salmon fishing nearly continuously for the better part of sixty years.

Fly fishing has been an important part of these sixty years, both as a form of recreation and as a business. There have been only two interruptions in my quest for *full-time* fishing however. The first was my tour of duty in the South Pacific and China with the Marine Corp during WWII. The other when I worked for thirty years with CH2M Hill, Engineers. The latter was much more enjoyable than my first diversion from fly fishing. It also enabled me to support my wife and five robin-mouthed offsprings. These working years also provided me the opportunity to work in close association with the finest professional and technical people in engineering.

After retiring from CH2M Hill, and finding retirement somewhat boring, I opened The Fly Fishers Place, a fly shop in the Central Oregon town of Sisters. Running the shop has been a most interesting, enjoyable and rewarding experience. It's allowed me to meet hundreds of wonderful people, fish with new friends, travel, explore fishing opportunities in other locations, and fulfill my lifelong dream of being involved in fly fishing on a full-time basis. I've also been able to record my fly fishing adventures in Oregon and now, through this guide, can offer you the benefit of these years of fly fishing and note-taking.

The Central and Southeast regions of Oregon, (commonly called the High Desert) are the origins of some of the most beautiful and pristine lakes and streams to be found anywhere in the world. Each region has its own distinct character and splendor. Some waters are bounded by old-growth forests of pine and fir, while others are surrounded by ancient junipers and desert vegetation.

When you're casting your fly to a rising trout, it is at times difficult to keep your concentration on fishing when the vistas beyond your quarry are the snow-covered peaks of the Cascade Mountains, the desert's wonderful rimrock canyons or the sheer magnitude of the Steens Mountain. The scenery is a photographers dream and a fly anglers haven.

The Central and Southeast regions also offer many opportunities for solitude. In most areas a short walk will take you into territory that is nearly undisturbed by human endeavors. Taking a break in the high desert country is a wonderful way to relax and rejuvenate your mind and body.

I believe you'll enjoy the fly fishing in this magnificent part of Oregon. More importantly, I think your fly fishing experiences in this area will *always* occupy a special place in your memory.

Introduction

In the Central and Southeast regions of Oregon, there are literally hundreds of lakes and reservoirs and miles and miles of rivers and creeks. I've not included all of these waters in this guide, but rather those that I've fished with success and those that are readily accessible to the public. I've also included comments on two private (with a fee) lakes, but only because I feel they're worth the price of admission.

A word on the ratings. Each river, stream, lake and reservoir in the main section of this guide has been rated on a scale from one to ten. A "ten" is water that offers the best possible fly fishing experience Oregon has to offer. A "one" would be fishable, but not much else.

These ratings are based on my experience fly fishing these waters over a *number* of years. Thus, my rating may not necessarily coincide with the experience you had on your particular day fly fishing, or even your combined experience. The best uses of these ratings are as a way to get a general idea of a particular fly fishing destination and as a means of comparing our opinions.

A word of advice. Get information. No matter where you're going fly fishing, there is a right time to be there, a right technique and a right fly pattern. Ask someone or check reputable literature (like this guide). Your best bet, in many cases, is to call a fly shop in the region. Several good ones are listed in the back of this guide. If you're still not getting the information you need, you can call me in Sisters, Oregon. My telephone number is in the book.

A word on words. Like it says on the cover, this is a "no nonsense" guide. When writing, I tried to eliminate a lot of small talk, flowery adjectives and unimportant falderal. This is an easy reading guide with essential and basic information. It will help you decide what water to visit and give you what you'll need to know to have a good time fly fishing. That being the case. . . on to the waters!

Section I

Some Thoughts on Fishing and Selected Rivers and Creeks

*M*y first experience on a fishing trip to Central Oregon was with my father in 1933. At that time we lived in Milwaukie, Oregon, which is southeast of Portland. While visiting a neighbor, we were shown large rainbow trout he'd recently caught in the Deschutes River. The image is still vivid, even though it was some sixty years ago when I was a boy of six. The following Sunday Dad got me up at 3:00 AM. We jumped in the pickup and headed for Maupin, a small community on the banks of the Deschutes about 100 miles east of home. I followed Dad up and down the river that day. When he hooked a fish he'd let me land it, or at least try. We didn't end up with the number or size of trout that we'd seen at our neighbors, but it was a memorable day. It provided me with a lasting memory of my Dad and it was the day I started my continuing love for the Deschutes River and the Central and Southeast regions of Oregon.

Since that first experience on the Deschutes River, I've fished the High Desert regions of Oregon hundreds of times. I've also had the good fortune to have fly fished from Argentina to Alaska. This has included the San Juan River in New Mexico, the Green River in Utah, the Wood in Idaho, and the Madison, Ruby and Beaverhead in Montana. But, if the truth be known, Central and Southeast Oregon compares favorably, and in many cases exceeds the fly fishing I found in most other parts of the lower forty-eight states.

When you're fishing Central and Southeast Oregon rivers, streams, lakes and reservoirs (or any place, for that matter) please practice conservation. Catch and release is a good way to start. And consider the five guidelines that all conscientious fly fishers obey:

- Abide by the laws
- Respect property owners rights
- Be considerate of others
- Never crowd in on another fisher
- Carry out your litter

Leaving an area better than you found it is the responsibility of all fly fishers. But enough of the obvious stuff. Here's hoping you hook that fish you've always dreamed of on one of the waters in this guide.

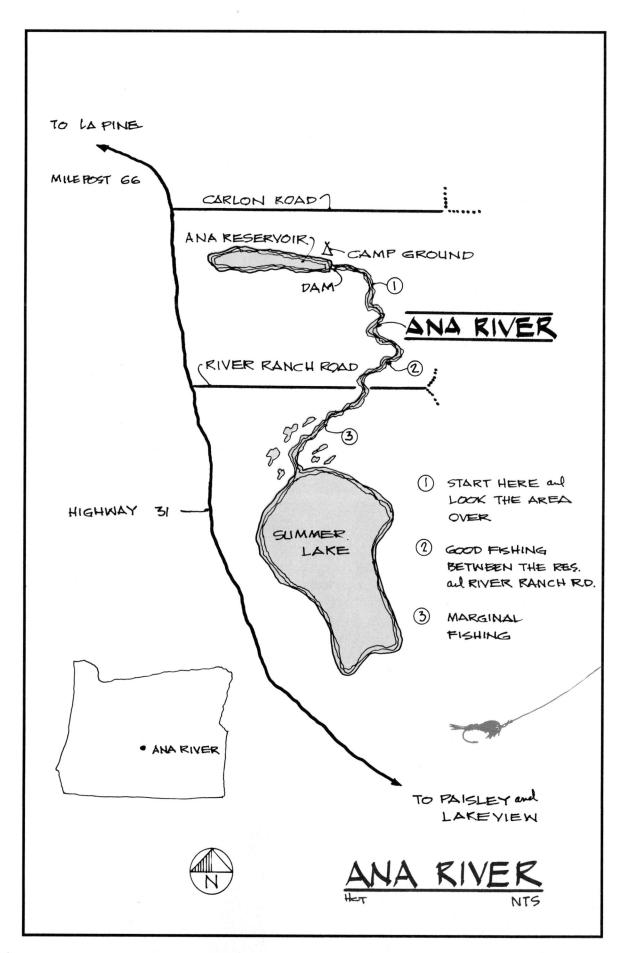

TO LA PINE

MILEPOST 66

CARLON ROAD

ANA RESERVOIR

CAMP GROUND

DAM

① **ANA RIVER**

RIVER RANCH ROAD

②

③

HIGHWAY 31

SUMMER LAKE

ANA RIVER

① START HERE and LOOK THE AREA OVER

② GOOD FISHING BETWEEN THE RES. and RIVER RANCH RD.

③ MARGINAL FISHING

TO PAISLEY and LAKEVIEW

N

ANA RIVER

HGT   NTS

The Ana River

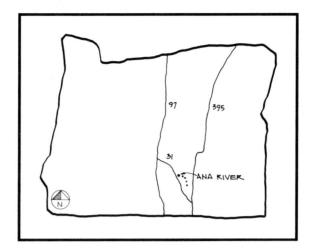

The Ana River lies easterly of Highway 31 near Summer Lake. This is an honest-to-God desert river. Its true origins are springs now covered by the Ana Reservoir. It flows through a sand and sagebrush landscape that is genuine Oregon High Desert. It flows from the Ana Reservoir and discharges into Summer Lake. It's only about seven miles long, doesn't get much pressure and holds some nice-sized rainbow trout. In a weekends time it is possible to fish the Ana River, Ana Reservoir, Lake of the Dunes and the Chewaucan River. I think you'll like the Ana River challenge of clear water and the need to make good fly presentations. See the suggestions on the accompanying map for some of the best places to fish the Ana.

Type of Fish
Mostly rainbow trout. These fish run from 8″ to 16″ and are great fighters.

Equipment to Use
Rods: 7′ to 9′ rods from 2 to 5 weight.
Line: Floating, to match rod weight.
Leaders: 5x and 6x, 9′ to 12′.
Reel: Palm drag.
Wading: neoprene waders with boots. You can fish much of this river without wading, however, I suggest you take the time to walk a quarter of a mile of it so you can determine if you want to wade. A wading staff is a good idea.

Flies to Use
You'll find an abundance of midges, mayflies and terrestrials around the river.
Dry patterns: Adams, Pale Morning Dun, Renegade, Spinner, Callibaetis, Comparadun and Blue Dun.
Nymphs: Hares Ear, Chironomid Pupa, Emerger and Zug Bug.

When to Fish
Best to fish in May-June and September-October. The Ana River fishes best in the early morning and late evening.

Seasons & Limits
The general trout season opens in late April and runs through the end of October. Because regulations are subject to change, consult the Oregon Department of Fish and Wildlife synopsis before fishing.

Accommodations & Services
There is a store, restaurant, motel and gas at Summer Lake. There are camping facilities near the dam at Ana Reservoir.

Harry's Opinion
The Ana River offers a unique fly fishing experience. You'll work for what you get, and at times it can be frustrating because you can't get a fish to rise. If you happen to hit one of those good days, you'll come back for more of the Ana.

Rating
A soft 4.

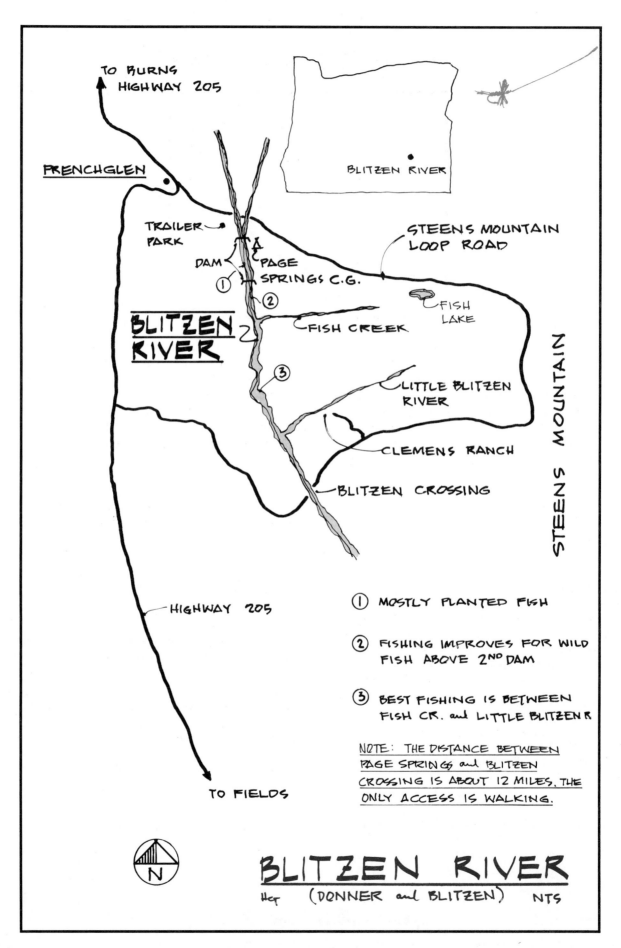

TO BURNS
HIGHWAY 205

FRENCHGLEN

BLITZEN RIVER

TRAILER
PARK

DAM

① PAGE
SPRINGS C.G.

②

STEENS MOUNTAIN
LOOP ROAD

FISH
LAKE

FISH CREEK

BLITZEN
RIVER

③

LITTLE BLITZEN
RIVER

CLEMENS RANCH

BLITZEN CROSSING

STEENS MOUNTAIN

HIGHWAY 205

TO FIELDS

① MOSTLY PLANTED FISH

② FISHING IMPROVES FOR WILD
   FISH ABOVE 2ND DAM

③ BEST FISHING IS BETWEEN
   FISH CR. and LITTLE BLITZEN R

NOTE: THE DISTANCE BETWEEN
PAGE SPRINGS and BLITZEN
CROSSING IS ABOUT 12 MILES. THE
ONLY ACCESS IS WALKING.

N

BLITZEN RIVER
HCT (DONNER and BLITZEN)   NTS

The Blitzen River

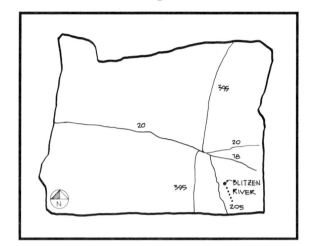

he Donner and Blitzen, commonly referred to as "The Blitzen" is located about 65 miles south of Burns, near the community of Frenchglen. Highway 205 from Burns to Frenchglen is paved. From Frenchglen to Page Springs campground the road is gravel.

The Blitzen has its origin in the Steens Mountains, one of the most beautiful and scenic regions in Oregon. This is a wonderful trout stream that requires lots of walking to get to the best fishing. The river above Page Springs flows through a relatively narrow canyon lined with juniper and pine trees. If you like small, remote, desert streams, then the Blitzen will fulfill one of your fly fishing fantasies. See the suggestions on the accompanying map for some of the best places to fish the Blitzen.

Type of Fish
Rainbow trout, from 8" to 14". However, fish up to 20" are taken on regular basis.

Equipment to Use
Rods: 1 to 5 weight rods, 6 ½' to 9'.
Line: Floating to match your rod weight.
Leaders: 4x and 5x leaders 9'.
Reel: Palm drag.
Wading: Since you will do a lot of walking, make sure your wading equipment is comfortable and fits properly. Here's what I do when fishing the Blitzen. . . I take the felt-soled, wading boots that I normally use with my neoprenes, put on a couple of pair of heavy socks (or neoprene socks) and wade in my everyday fishing pants. Yes, I get wet up to my thighs, but on a hot day in the Blitzen Canyon, the cool water is a welcome relief.

Flies to Use
Depending on the time of year you fish the Blitzen, you'll find you'll need to adapt your pattern selection to what's happening on the river. There is one fly I've found that fishes well, regardless of the time of year, the Royal Wulff size #14.
Dry patterns: Royal Wulff, Comparadun, Elk Hair Caddis, Adams, Hopper, Renegade and Humpy.
Nymphs & streamers: Wooly Worm, Prince, Hares Ear, Muddler and Sculpin.

When to Fish
Fishing the Blitzen from mid-July through October has been best for me. April and May fishing can be OK but, depending on runoff, the river can be high and out of shape. Fishing in the late afternoon and evening is generally most productive.

Season & Limits
The Blitzen opens in late April and closes the end of October. Check the ODFW synopsis for exact dates and limits.

Accommodations & Services
At Frenchglen, there is a small hotel with food service, a store, gas, and not much else. At Page Springs, there is a wonderful Bureau of Land Management campground. A private trailer park is located near Page Springs campground which has limited supplies and rents trailers for overnight accommodations.

Harry's Opinion
I'm one happy person when I'm fishing the Blitzen. If I could design my own trout stream, I'd use the Blitzen above Page Springs as a model. In my opinion, the Blitzen is a delicate resource that needs our protection. It can stand a reasonable amount of fishing and recreational pressure if we all practice intelligent conservation. I strongly recommend you practice catch and release on this stream.

Rating
A strong 6.5.

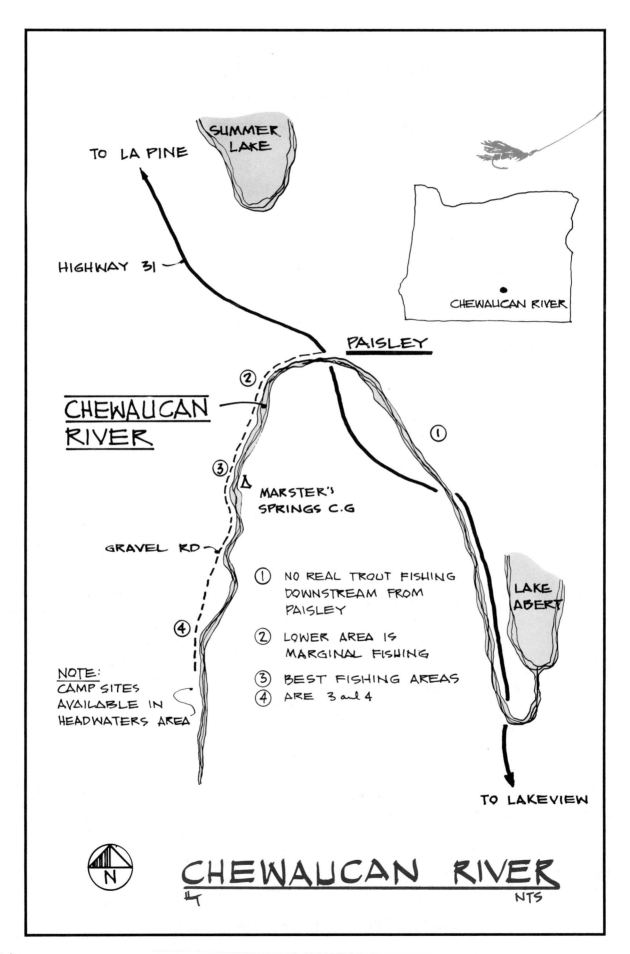

TO LA PINE

SUMMER LAKE

HIGHWAY 31

PAISLEY

CHEWAUCAN RIVER

CHEWAUCAN RIVER

②

③

④

MARSTER'S SPRINGS C.G

GRAVEL RD

① NO REAL TROUT FISHING DOWNSTREAM FROM PAISLEY

② LOWER AREA IS MARGINAL FISHING

③ BEST FISHING AREAS
④ ARE 3 and 4

①

LAKE ABERT

NOTE: CAMP SITES AVAILABLE IN HEADWATERS AREA

TO LAKEVIEW

N

CHEWAUCAN RIVER

NTS

The Chewaucan River

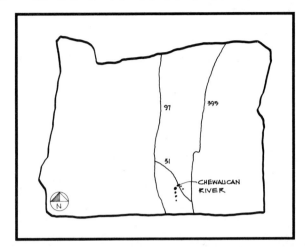

T he Chewaucan is near the town of Paisley, on Highway 31. You'll need to turn to the south, just west of Paisley, to access the best fishing part of the river. The Chewaucan flows out of the mountains and heads for the Great Basin, where it dissipates into the Oregon desert. As you go upstream from Paisley you enter the Fremont National Forest. Much of the river lies in this pine forest. It is not a big river, but one that is enjoyable to fish. See the suggestions on the accompanying map for some of the best places to fish the Chewaucan.

Type of Fish
Predominantly planted rainbow trout from 8″ to 12″, however, there are some nice fish in the 14″ to 16″ range taken on a regular basis.

Equipment to Use
Rods: 3, 4 and 5 weight, 7½′ to 9′.
Line: Match floating and sink tip to rod weight.
Leaders: 4x and 5x, 9′.
Reel: Palm drag.
Wading: Felt-soled hip boots are OK, but you'll be better off with waist-high neoprenes with felt-soled wading shoes. And don't forget mosquito repellent. You'll need it!

Flies to Use
Dry patterns: Pale Morning Dun, Adams, Renegade, Royal Wulff, Mosquito, Comparadun and Elk Hair Caddis.
Nymphs: Pheasant Tail, Hares Ear, Zug Bug and Caddis Pupa.

When to Fish
Regulars on the Chewaucan seem to prefer July through October. Late afternoon and evening are generally the best times to fish.

Season & Limits
The Chewaucan opens in late April and closes in late October. Consult the ODFW synopsis for exact dates and limits.

Harry's Opinion
I like the Chewaucan. It's a nice river to fish, off the beaten path, and not overcrowded. Even though it's not a highly rated stream, I feel it's worth the trip. Exploring new territory is part of the fun of fly fishing.

Rating
The Chewaucan is a 4. If you hit "One of those days," it can be an 8 or 9.

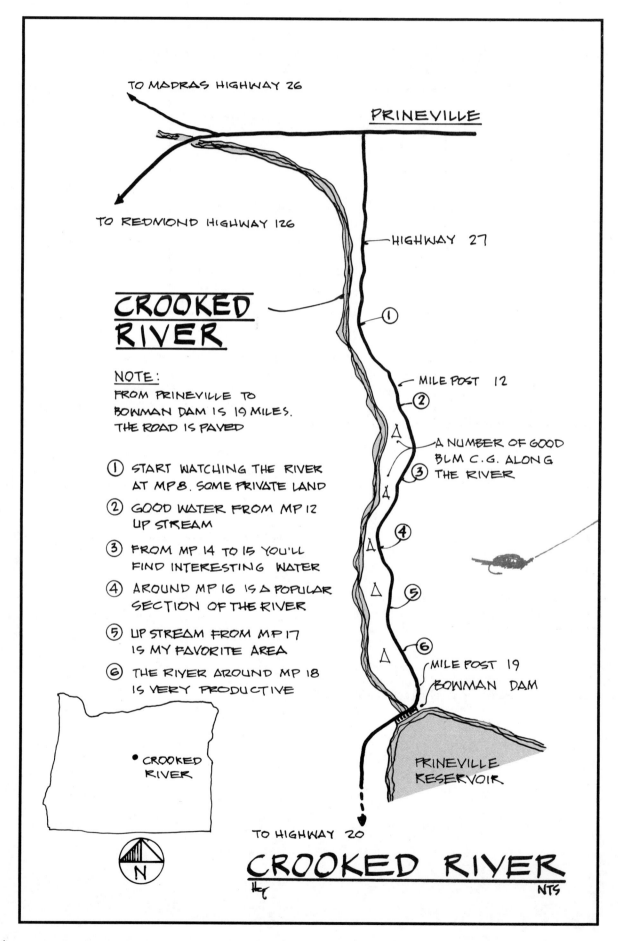

TO MADRAS HIGHWAY 26

PRINEVILLE

TO REDMOND HIGHWAY 126

HIGHWAY 27

CROOKED RIVER

NOTE:
FROM PRINEVILLE TO
BOWMAN DAM IS 19 MILES.
THE ROAD IS PAVED

① START WATCHING THE RIVER
AT MP 8. SOME PRIVATE LAND

② GOOD WATER FROM MP 12
UP STREAM

③ FROM MP 14 TO 15 YOU'LL
FIND INTERESTING WATER

④ AROUND MP 16 IS A POPULAR
SECTION OF THE RIVER

⑤ UP STREAM FROM MP 17
IS MY FAVORITE AREA

⑥ THE RIVER AROUND MP 18
IS VERY PRODUCTIVE

①

MILE POST 12

②

A NUMBER OF GOOD
BLM C.G. ALONG
THE RIVER

③

④

⑤

⑥

MILE POST 19
BOWMAN DAM

PRINEVILLE
RESERVOIR

• CROOKED
RIVER

TO HIGHWAY 20

N

CROOKED RIVER

NTS

The Crooked River

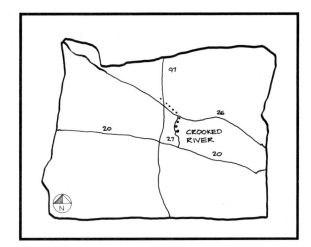

The primary fishing section of the Crooked River lies south of the city of Prineville. From Prineville to Bowman Dam, 19 miles, Highway 27 is paved and parallels the river.

The Crooked River below Bowman Dam is a wonderful tailrace stream, that is, it's wonderful when the Bureau of Reclamation releases an adequate amount of water (minimum of 75 cfs) to truly sustain this quality fishery. The geographical features are impressive. High basalt walls and juniper, pine and sage-covered flats create an environment right out of a wild west movie set. Most of the time the water is off color, but don't let that bother you, it doesn't seem to bother the fish. See the suggestions on the accompanying map for some of the best places to fish the Crooked River.

Type of Fish

Rainbows, cutthroats and a rainbow-cutthroat cross. Most fish will run from 8″ to 12″, but you'll get a fair number in the 13″ to 18″ range. We've seen pictures of 6 plus pound fish, but I haven't hooked one.

Equipment to Use

Rods: 1 to 5 weight.
Line: Match to rod weight. Though a great nymphing stream, floating lines with weighted nymphs will produce.
Leaders: 4x and 5x leaders, 9′. When nymphing use a strike indicator.
Reel: Palm drag.
Wading: The Crooked is not necessarily difficult to wade if you use good judgment, *but it's tricky.* There are lots of boulders that can cause embarrassing problems, not life threatening, but obstacles that can make you look like an unskilled gymnast. I suggest you have felt-soled, wading shoes, a wading staff and at least waist-high neopenes.

Flies to Use

From mile post 12 to 19, which is really the prime area, you'll find some interesting water. The basic food of the fish here is a fresh water shrimp that's in the river by the zillions.
Dry patterns: Adams, Comparadun, Elk Hair Caddis and Renegade.

Nymphs: Scuds, Hares Ear, Scuds, Pheasant Tail, Scuds, Wooly Worm and Scuds. Also try Scuds.

When to Fish

The Crooked is open year-round, so you should fish it whenever you've got the time. However, there are times in the winter months when the Crooked is frozen over, so check first. In my opinion the Crooked fishes well all day long, with the best time in the late afternoon and evening.

Season & Limits

The Crooked is open year round, but the season is subject to change (like most regulations). There are restrictions on fish limits and fishing methods. Refer to the ODFW synopsis before fishing.

Accommodations & Services

There are fine camping areas provided by the BLM all along the river. Lodging can be found in Prineville. There is a full range of services available in Prineville including restaurants, groceries, lodging, gas and automotive services.

Harry's Opinion

I like the Crooked River from mile post 12 to 18. There are plenty of fish and it's a good stream for all skill levels.

Rating

A 6.5.

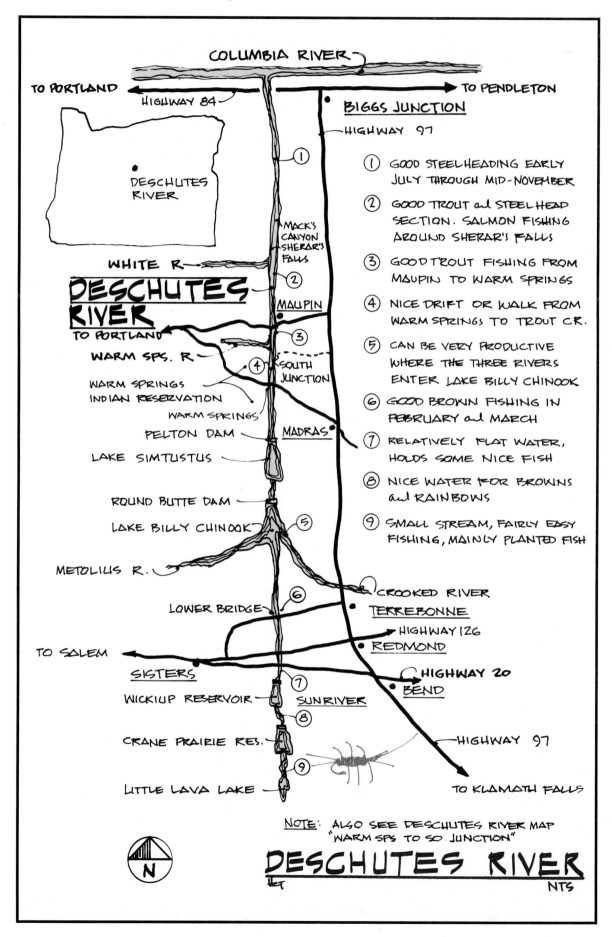

COLUMBIA RIVER

TO PORTLAND — HIGHWAY 84 — TO PENDLETON

BIGGS JUNCTION

HIGHWAY 97

DESCHUTES RIVER

WHITE R.

DESCHUTES RIVER
TO PORTLAND

WARM SPS. R.

WARM SPRINGS INDIAN RESERVATION

WARM SPRINGS

PELTON DAM

LAKE SIMTUSTUS

ROUND BUTTE DAM

LAKE BILLY CHINOOK

METOLIUS R.

LOWER BRIDGE

TO SALEM

SISTERS

WICKIUP RESERVOIR

CRANE PRAIRIE RES.

LITTLE LAVA LAKE

MACK'S CANYON
SHERAR'S FALLS

MAUPIN

SOUTH JUNCTION

MADRAS

CROOKED RIVER

TERREBONNE

HIGHWAY 126

REDMOND

HIGHWAY 20

BEND

HIGHWAY 97

SUNRIVER

TO KLAMATH FALLS

① GOOD STEELHEADING EARLY JULY THROUGH MID-NOVEMBER

② GOOD TROUT and STEELHEAD SECTION. SALMON FISHING AROUND SHERAR'S FALLS

③ GOOD TROUT FISHING FROM MAUPIN TO WARM SPRINGS

④ NICE DRIFT OR WALK FROM WARM SPRINGS TO TROUT CR.

⑤ CAN BE VERY PRODUCTIVE WHERE THE THREE RIVERS ENTER LAKE BILLY CHINOOK

⑥ GOOD BROWN FISHING IN FEBRUARY and MARCH

⑦ RELATIVELY FLAT WATER, HOLDS SOME NICE FISH

⑧ NICE WATER FOR BROWNS and RAINBOWS

⑨ SMALL STREAM, FAIRLY EASY FISHING, MAINLY PLANTED FISH

NOTE: ALSO SEE DESCHUTES RIVER MAP "WARM SPS TO SO. JUNCTION"

N

DESCHUTES RIVER

NTS

The Deschutes River

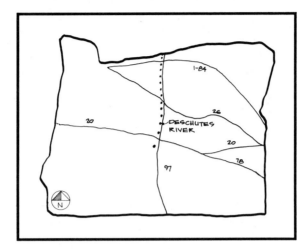

*T*he Deschutes River lies east of the Cascade Mountains and runs from its source at Little Lava Lake (west, southwest, of Bend), in a northerly direction until it flows into the Columbia River east of The Dalles. The river setting changes from mature pine forests to sheer basalt canyons with desert vegetation.

The Deschutes is probably the finest overall fishing river in Western America. With its complement of trout, salmon, steelhead and whitefish, it offers a wide range of quality angling for the fly fisher. See the suggestions on the accompanying map for some of the best places to fish the Deschutes.

Type of Fish

Predominantly rainbow trout, with some bull trout (Dolly Varden), and browns. Salmon and steelhead are available during their spawning runs. The Deschutes summer-run steelhead is a world-class fish!! There is also an abundance of whitefish. Don't take this fish lightly, it can supply you with some very exciting fishing.

Equipment to Use

The Deschutes, for the most part, is "Big River." From its source to Crane Prairie Reservoir, the Deschutes is a relatively small meandering stream. Upon leaving Wickiup Reservoir it becomes a full-flowing river. Since the vast majority of the quality fishing is located on the Big River, I'll address equipment needs to that portion.

TROUT
Rods: 4 to 7 weight rods, 8½' to 9½'.
Line: Both floating and sink tip lines to match rod weight.
Leaders: 4x and 5x, 9' for dry flies. 4x, 7' to 9' for nymphing, use a strike indicator.
Reel: Palm drag.

STEELHEAD
Rods: 6 to 9 weight, 8½' to 9½'.
Line: Both floating and sink tip to match rod weight.
Leaders: 0x or 1x, 7' to 9'.
Reel: Mechanical drag.
Wading: Wading the Deschutes is always a challenge. You'll need chest-high neoprenes with felt-soled wading shoes or stream cleats and a wading staff. Use your best wading sense when wading in the Deschutes!

Flies to Use

You'll find a full range of midges, mayflies, caddis, stones and terrestrials that feed the Deschutes fish. The secret to feeding them something that has your hook on it is being there at the right time with the right flies. Starting at the opening of trout season in late April, until the season closes at the end of October, you can fish with a variety of nymphs.

The dry fly action starts picking up by the middle of May and continues through the close of the season. Late May through mid-June is the salmon fly hatch, followed by an exceptional caddis and mayfly hatch, which lasts well into September. In October the caddis goes into its act.

Dry patterns: Adams, Elk Hair Caddis, Comparadun, Pale Morning Dun, Renegade, Salmon Flies and October Caddis.
Nymphs: Girdle Bug, Hares Ear, Kaufman Stone, Sparkle Pupa and Feather Duster.
Steelhead: Green Butted Skunk, Skunk, Macks Canyon, Purple Peril and Silver Hilton. Don't tie your Steelhead flies too full. A little on the sparse side (low water ties) seems to get the best results. Let me suggest that you have #14, #16 and #18 Black Stones for winter fishing in the vicinity of Lower Bridge. On any given day you can experience some exceptional brown trout fishing.

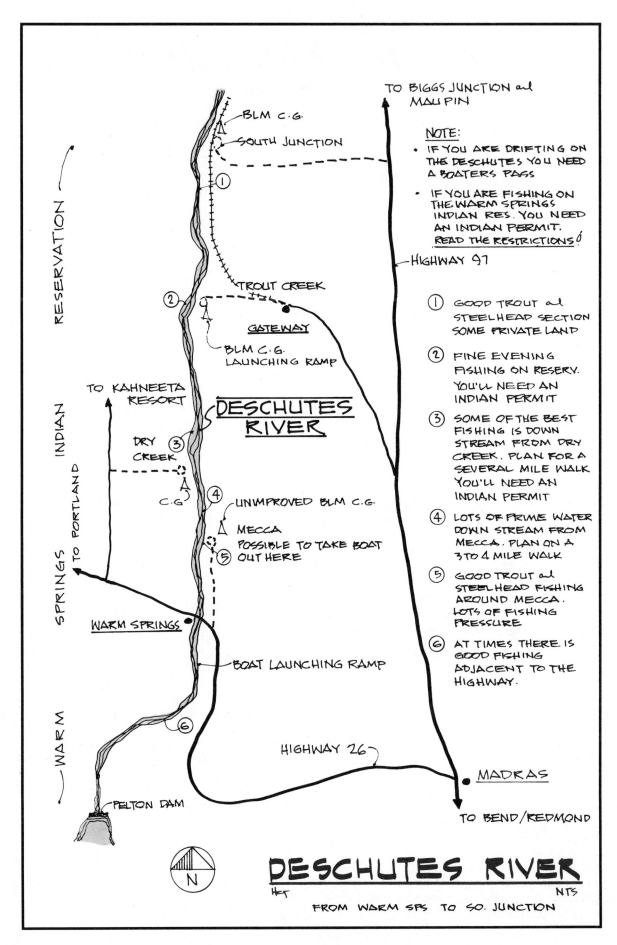

TO BIGGS JUNCTION and MAUPIN

BLM C.G.

SOUTH JUNCTION

RESERVATION

NOTE:
- IF YOU ARE DRIFTING ON THE DESCHUTES YOU NEED A BOATERS PASS
- IF YOU ARE FISHING ON THE WARM SPRINGS INDIAN RES. YOU NEED AN INDIAN PERMIT. READ THE RESTRICTIONS

HIGHWAY 97

① GOOD TROUT and STEELHEAD SECTION SOME PRIVATE LAND

TROUT CREEK

GATEWAY

BLM C.G. LAUNCHING RAMP

② FINE EVENING FISHING ON RESERV. YOU'LL NEED AN INDIAN PERMIT

TO KAHNEETA RESORT

DESCHUTES RIVER

INDIAN

③ SOME OF THE BEST FISHING IS DOWN STREAM FROM DRY CREEK. PLAN FOR A SEVERAL MILE WALK YOU'LL NEED AN INDIAN PERMIT

DRY CREEK

TO PORTLAND

C.G

④ UNIMPROVED BLM C.G.

④ LOTS OF PRIME WATER DOWN STREAM FROM MECCA. PLAN ON A 3 TO 4 MILE WALK

MECCA POSSIBLE TO TAKE BOAT OUT HERE

⑤ GOOD TROUT and STEELHEAD FISHING AROUND MECCA. LOTS OF FISHING PRESSURE

SPRINGS

⑥ AT TIMES THERE IS GOOD FISHING ADJACENT TO THE HIGHWAY.

WARM SPRINGS

BOAT LAUNCHING RAMP

WARM

HIGHWAY 26

MADRAS

PELTON DAM

TO BEND/REDMOND

N

DESCHUTES RIVER

HT   NTS

FROM WARM SPS TO SO. JUNCTION

When to Fish

On the Deschutes, trout fish whenever you can. Evening fishing is far and away the best time. I suggest you consider the salmon fly hatch in early June; the caddis and mayfly hatch in late September and October. For steelheading, the best fishing generally starts where the Deschutes empties into the Columbia River (the mouth) about mid-July, with the majority of fish being taken from the mouth to Sherars Falls. From September until the season closes, good steelheading can be had from above Sherars Falls to Pelton Dam.

Season & Limits

The fishing season, and limits, vary on the Deschutes and are subject to frequent changes. Consult ODFW synopsis before fishing.

Accommodations & Services

On the upper river, above Bend, there are accommodations at Sunriver and South Twin Lake and, near Bend, there are a number of resorts and motels. In the central section of the river, from Bend to Madras, there are motels at Redmond and Madras and a fine resort at Eagle Crest, just west of Redmond. On the lower section of the Deschutes, from Madras (Warm Springs) to the mouth at the Columbia River, there are resort accommodations at Kahneeta. The Kahneeta Resort is located on the Warm Springs Indian Reservation. If you stay there, you can fish a section of the Warm Springs River. There are also accommodations at Maupin. If you're fishing near the mouth of the Deschutes, there are motels, restaurant, groceries and gas at Biggs Junction. There is a full range of services from Bend to Maupin. From Macks Canyon to the mouth, about 25 miles, the river is accessed only by walking or boat. (The only exception is a primitive road to the river at Kloan.) You'd better have everything you need in this section because there isn't a corner Seven-Eleven.

Harry's Opinion

If I only had one river to fish, the Deschutes would be it. It has it all: beauty, variety of fish, challenging water and a true test of fly fishing skills. Yet, it's possible to take a real neophyte to the river and, with some assistance, get him or her into fish.

Rating

The Deschutes River is as close to a 10 as you'll find in Oregon and the West.

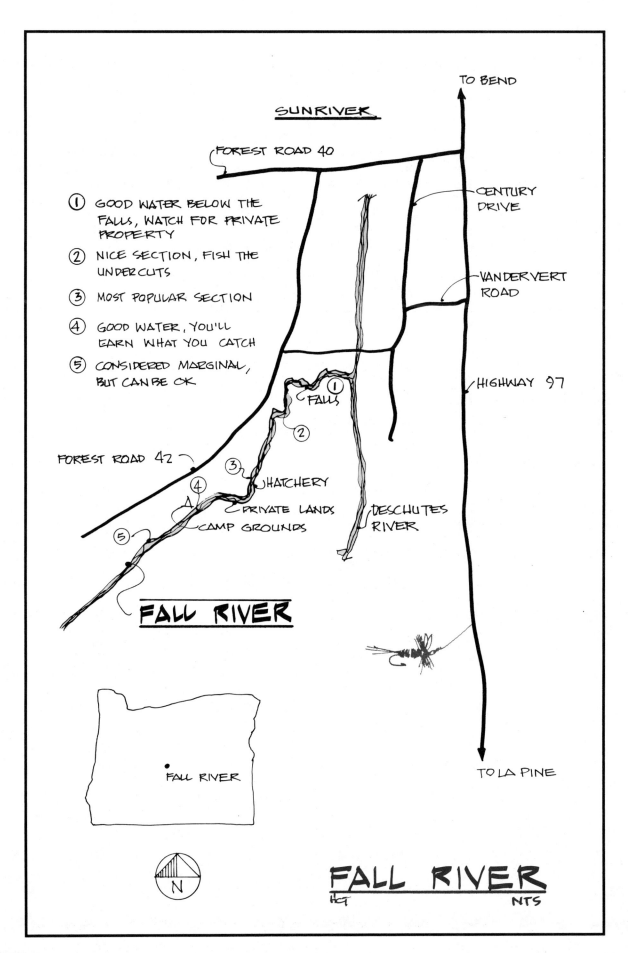

SUNRIVER

TO BEND

FOREST ROAD 40

CENTURY DRIVE

① GOOD WATER BELOW THE FALLS, WATCH FOR PRIVATE PROPERTY

② NICE SECTION, FISH THE UNDERCUTS

③ MOST POPULAR SECTION

④ GOOD WATER, YOU'LL EARN WHAT YOU CATCH

⑤ CONSIDERED MARGINAL, BUT CAN BE OK

VANDERVERT ROAD

HIGHWAY 97

FALLS ①

②

FOREST ROAD 42

③

④

⑤

HATCHERY

PRIVATE LANDS

CAMP GROUNDS

DESCHUTES RIVER

FALL RIVER

FALL RIVER

TO LA PINE

N

FALL RIVER
HCG   NTS

Fall River

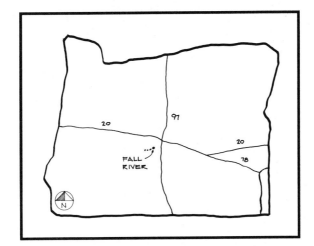

The Fall River is about 25 miles southwest of Bend. It is readily accessible off Century Drive. Its close proximity to Sunriver and the population center of Bend makes it a popular destination for local fly fishers.

Fall River is approximately 10 miles long, its origin being a spring below Wickiup Reservoir. It flows through a pine forest and ultimately empties into the Deschutes River between Sunriver and La Pine. During the mosquito season, be sure to have a good repellent.

You'll like the geographic features of the area, from the gentle rolling hills of the pine forest to the massive rock outcroppings that are scattered across the landscape. The river is very clear and cold, making it necessary to make good presentations when casting and making yourself invisible while doing so. See the suggestions on the accompanying map for some of the best places to fish Fall River.

Type of Fish
Rainbow, brook and brown trout . The majority will run 8" to 12".

Equipment to Use
Rods: 1 to 5 weights, 6½' to 9'.
Line: Floating line to match your rod weight.
Leaders: 5x to 7x, 9' to 15' depending on where you're fishing and climate.
Reel: Palm drag.
Wading: Neoprene waders with felt-soled wading shoes and a wading staff.

Flies to Use
The Fall River hatches are mainly midges, caddis, mayflies and terrestrials. You'll find that some combination of the following patterns will take fish.
Dry patterns: Adams, Renegade, Comparadun, Pale Morning Dun, Olive Dun, and Elk Hair Caddis.
Nymphs: Pheasant Tail, Hares Ear, Sparkle Pupa, Zug Bug and Soft Hackle.

When to Fish
The Fall River fishing holds up pretty well all year because of the ODFW stocking program. Most Fall River enthusiasts like late June, July and August. Evening hours generally produce the best results.

Season & Limits
The Fall River opens in late April and closes the end of October. Refer to the ODFW synopsis for exact dates and limits.

Accommodations & Services
There are good camp sites available along the river. Sunriver, Bend and La Pine all have accommodations and all are within a half-hour drive to the river. Stores, restaurants, gas and groceries are available in these locations.

Harry's Opinion
You'll like the challenge of the Fall River. It takes good presentation. Good polarizing glasses will help you spot the fish here. This spring creek type river isn't for everyone, but for those who enjoy light equipment and the challenge of delicate presentation, the Fall River is on the fly fishers' *must* list.

Rating
Fall River is a high end 5.

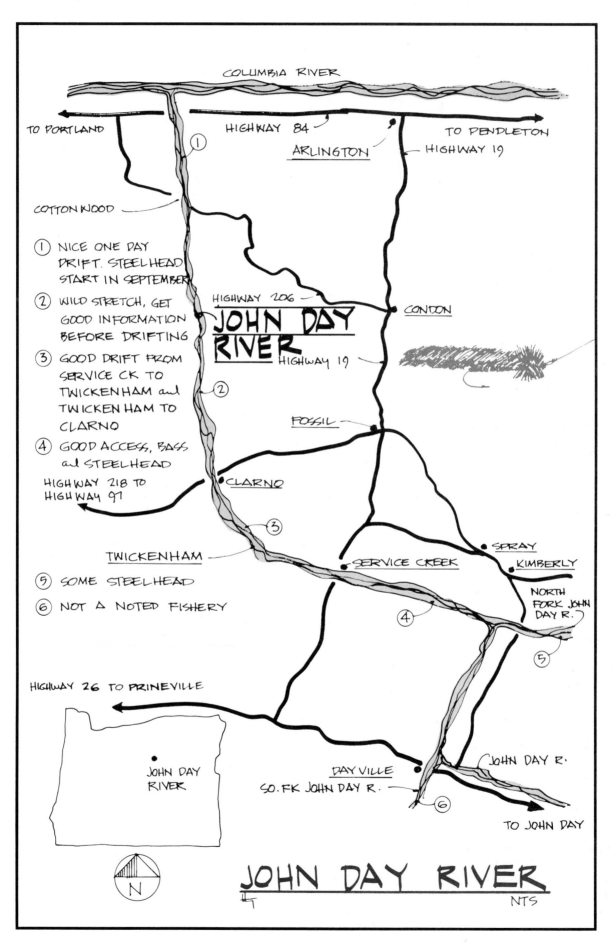

COLUMBIA RIVER

TO PORTLAND   HIGHWAY 84   TO PENDLETON
① ARLINGTON   HIGHWAY 19

COTTONWOOD

① NICE ONE DAY
   DRIFT. STEELHEAD
   START IN SEPTEMBER

② WILD STRETCH, GET
   GOOD INFORMATION
   BEFORE DRIFTING

③ GOOD DRIFT FROM
   SERVICE CK TO
   TWICKENHAM and
   TWICKENHAM TO
   CLARNO

④ GOOD ACCESS, BASS
   and STEELHEAD

HIGHWAY 218 TO
HIGHWAY 97

HIGHWAY 206
JOHN DAY RIVER
HIGHWAY 19   CONDON

FOSSIL

CLARNO

③

TWICKENHAM

⑤ SOME STEELHEAD

⑥ NOT A NOTED FISHERY

SPRAY
SERVICE CREEK   KIMBERLY

NORTH
FORK JOHN
DAY R.

④

⑤

HIGHWAY 26 TO PRINEVILLE

JOHN DAY
RIVER

DAYVILLE   JOHN DAY R.
SO. FK JOHN DAY R.

⑥

TO JOHN DAY

N

JOHN DAY RIVER
NTS

❖ 16 ❖

The John Day River

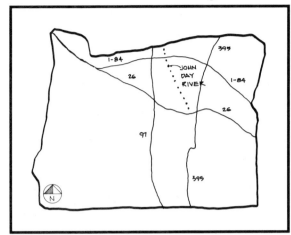

The John Day River, in the eastern portion of Central Oregon, runs from above the town of John Day north to the Columbia River. If you like semi-arid landscape, you'll fall in love with the John Day River. There are lots of access points between Kimberly and Service Creek, but for the next 100 or so miles below Service Creek access is really limited. Drifting below Clarno can be tricky. See the suggestions on the accompanying map for some of the best places to fish. The John Day is the only major stream in the Columbia drainage system in Oregon without a hydroelectric project blocking migratory fish.

Type of Fish
You'll find rainbow trout, steelhead and bass in the John Day system. Several years ago the ODFW biologist responsible for the John Day River drainage stated that the native steelhead run in the river was the largest in Oregon. He indicated approximately 26,000 of these fish were observed on the spawning beds.

Equipment to Use
You'll need a variety of equipment depending on the time of year. Here are general guidelines.

TROUT
Rods: 4 to 7 weight, 8½' to 9'.
Line: Floating and sink tip to match rod weight.
Leaders: 3x to 5x, 7½' to 9'.
Reel: Palm drag.

STEELHEAD
Rods: 6 to 9 weight, 8½' to 9'.
Line: Floating and sink tip to match rod weight.
Leaders: 1x to 3x, 7' to 9'.
Reel: Mechanical drag.
Wading: Chest-high neoprenes with felt-soled wading shoes or stream cleats and a wading staff. If you are planning to float below Clarno, consult a qualified and knowledgeable guide.

Flies to Use
This is a tough one since you can fish for trout, bass and steelhead; however, my experience suggests the following:
Dry patterns: Adams, Renegade, various mayfly patterns.

Nymphs & streamers: Wooly Worm, Hares Ear, Matuka, Muddler, Zonker and Wooly Buggers.
Steelhead: Skunks, Green Butted Skunk, Red Wing Blackbird and Silver Hilton.

When to Fish
Because water flows vary dramatically I suggest that you consult a qualified guide. Fish for bass May through August and hit the steelhead during the late fall and winter months.

Season & Limits
Since the season and limits vary on the John Day River system, it is important that you refer to the ODFW synopsis for current regulations.

Accommodations & Services
You'll find, along the accessible length of the John Day River, rather limited accommodations and related facilities. Restaurants, service stations and groceries are concentrated downstream from Kimberly. There are some nice camp sites between Kimberly and Service Creek.

Harry's Opinion
The John Day can range from a 2 to a 6 depending on when you fish the river. I suggest you take the time to carefully evaluate the steelhead fishery on this river.

Rating
Trout, a 2. Bass, a 6. Steelhead, a strong 5.

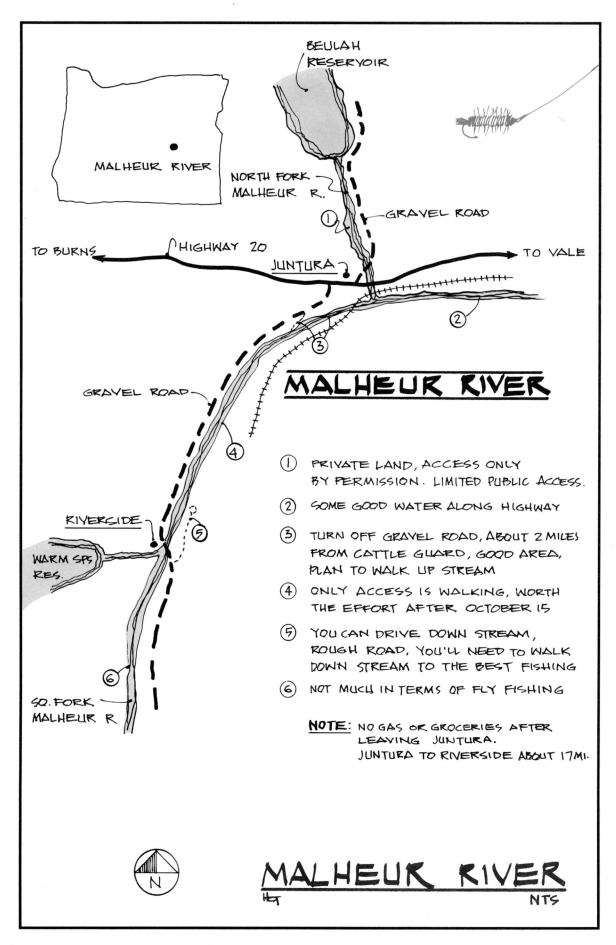

BEULAH RESERVOIR

MALHEUR RIVER

NORTH FORK MALHEUR R.

GRAVEL ROAD

①

TO BURNS — HIGHWAY 20 — TO VALE

JUNTURA

②

③

MALHEUR RIVER

GRAVEL ROAD

④

RIVERSIDE

⑤

WARM SPS RES.

⑥

SO. FORK MALHEUR R

① PRIVATE LAND, ACCESS ONLY BY PERMISSION. LIMITED PUBLIC ACCESS.

② SOME GOOD WATER ALONG HIGHWAY

③ TURN OFF GRAVEL ROAD, ABOUT 2 MILES FROM CATTLE GUARD, GOOD AREA, PLAN TO WALK UP STREAM

④ ONLY ACCESS IS WALKING, WORTH THE EFFORT AFTER OCTOBER 15

⑤ YOU CAN DRIVE DOWN STREAM, ROUGH ROAD, YOU'LL NEED TO WALK DOWN STREAM TO THE BEST FISHING

⑥ NOT MUCH IN TERMS OF FLY FISHING

NOTE: NO GAS OR GROCERIES AFTER LEAVING JUNTURA. JUNTURA TO RIVERSIDE ABOUT 17 MI.

N

MALHEUR RIVER

HCT   NTS

The Malheur River

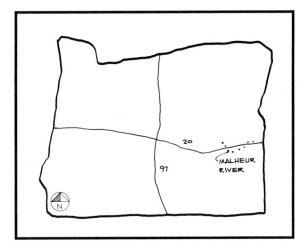

The Malheur River is located in the eastern part of Oregon and flows from the Strawberry Range to the Snake River on the Oregon-Idaho border. The Malheur is subject to water fluctuations brought about by winter precipitation and irrigation demands. In good water years, the main stem of the Malheur and its tributaries offer some of the finest trout fishing I've ever experienced. Watch the water conditions on this superb stream. When its not being used as an irrigation conduit, you can experience some of the best desert trout fishing in Oregon. See the suggestions on the accompanying map for some of the best places to fish the Malheur.

Type of Fish
The Malheur is a rainbow fishery. When the river has adequate stream flows and the trout population is healthy, I can't think of a stream I'd rather fish.

Equipment to Use
You don't have to be very sophisticated on the Malheur.
Rods: 3 to 6 weight.
Line: Floating line to match rod weight.
Leaders: 4x, 5x and 6x, 9'.
Reel: Palm drag.
Wading: Lots of walking here, so use "light" wading equipment. Hip boots are fine, or simply wear wading shoes and light weight pants.

Flies to Use
Dry patterns: Hopper, Comparadun, Renegade, Adams and Elk Hair Caddis.
Nymphs & streamers: Hares Ear, Wooly Worm, Muddler and Sculpin.

When to Fish
The quality fishing on the Malheur is usually after the 15th of October. This is when the river ceases to be an irrigation conduit for the rich farm land of the Treasure Valley. I like to fish the Malheur from Riverside to about 10 miles below Juntura from mid-October until the winter weather makes you seek a warm fire and a good book.

Season & Limits
The Malheur River is open all year; however, regulations and limits are subject to change, so refer to the ODFW synopsis for current information.

Accommodations & Services
There are limited facilities in the fishable area of the Malheur. Juntura has a motel, gas, groceries and two restaurants.

Harry's Opinion
I've spent many wonderful fall days on the Malheur with my wife and friends. We mostly fish, but we also hunt chukar. If you're looking for a place to spend a delightful fall, both fly fishing and bird hunting, take a fling at the Malheur between Riverside and Juntura.

Rating
The Malheur, in the fall or spring, when the water is right, is a 7. During the summer, when it's an irrigation conduit, it's a 1.

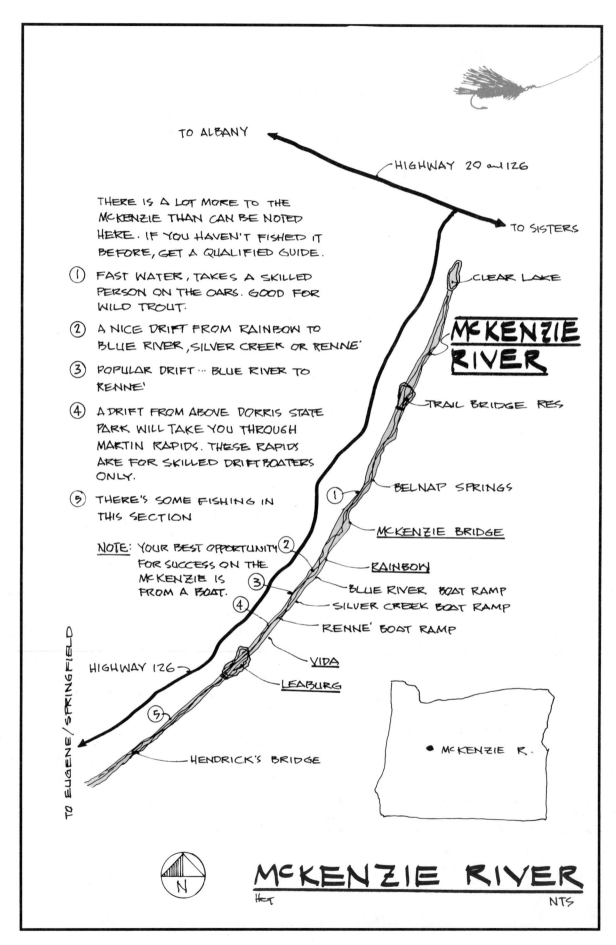

TO ALBANY

HIGHWAY 20 and 126

TO SISTERS

THERE IS A LOT MORE TO THE McKENZIE THAN CAN BE NOTED HERE. IF YOU HAVEN'T FISHED IT BEFORE, GET A QUALIFIED GUIDE.

① FAST WATER, TAKES A SKILLED PERSON ON THE OARS. GOOD FOR WILD TROUT.

② A NICE DRIFT FROM RAINBOW TO BLUE RIVER, SILVER CREEK OR RENNE'

③ POPULAR DRIFT … BLUE RIVER TO RENNE'

④ A DRIFT FROM ABOVE DORRIS STATE PARK WILL TAKE YOU THROUGH MARTIN RAPIDS. THESE RAPIDS ARE FOR SKILLED DRIFT BOATERS ONLY.

⑤ THERE'S SOME FISHING IN THIS SECTION

NOTE: YOUR BEST OPPORTUNITY FOR SUCCESS ON THE McKENZIE IS FROM A BOAT.

CLEAR LAKE

McKENZIE RIVER

TRAIL BRIDGE RES.

BELNAP SPRINGS

McKENZIE BRIDGE

RAINBOW

BLUE RIVER BOAT RAMP
SILVER CREEK BOAT RAMP
RENNE' BOAT RAMP

VIDA

HIGHWAY 126

LEABURG

TO EUGENE/SPRINGFIELD

HENDRICK'S BRIDGE

McKENZIE R.

N

McKENZIE RIVER

HCT   NTS

The McKenzie River

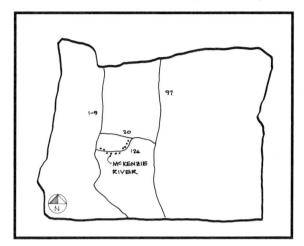

*T*ravel west of Sisters on Highway 26 about 50 miles and you will come to the best fishing section on the McKenzie. All weather Highway 26, parallels the river from its source at Clear Lake to Eugene.

The McKenzie is one of the most beautiful rivers in the west. The McKenzie drift boat originated on this river, a boat type which is now used world-wide. President Hoover spent much of his fishing life on the McKenzie, but so have a lot of other people. See the suggestions on the accompanying map for some of the best places to fish the McKenzie.

Type of Fish
Rainbow trout, steelhead and salmon call the McKenzie home. There are two types of rainbows: stocked and native. The native fish are referred to as redsides. The stocked fish (the majority) run from 8″ to 12″. The Redsides range from 12″ to 20″.

Equipment to Use
Rods: 5, 6 and 7 weight, 8½′ to 9½′.
Line: For trout, either a floating or sink tip line will serve you, though you'll probably use your floating line the majority of the time.
Leader: When fishing dry, 4x, 5x or 6x, 9′. For nymphs use 7½′ with a strike indicator.
Reel: Mechanical and palm drag.
Wading: Not many good wading areas. They are isolated and one must search for them. Best to drift this stream.

Flies to Use
The McKenzie has hatches of midges, caddis, mayflies, some stones and terrestrials. When the season opens in late April, the dry fly activity is just starting.
Dry patterns: Adams, Renegade, Royal Wulff, Humpy, Elk Hair Caddis and Comparadun. I've seen October Caddis patterns work well when the stones are hatching.
Nymphs: Prince, Hares Ear, Sparkle Pupa and Pheasant Tail.
Steelhead: Skunks, Green Butted Skunk and Silver Hilton.

When to Fish
The heavyweight guides like the river best from late May to early September. You can generally catch fish all day long because there are always some sections of the river in shadow.

Seasons & Limits
The river is open from late April to the end of October. For exact dates and limits, refer to the ODFW synopsis.

Accommodations & Services
There are numerous good resorts and motels located on or adjacent to the river. Stores, restaurants, gas stations and auto repair garages are located from McKenzie Bridge to Walterville. For those not fishing, there's excellent golfing nearby at the Tokatee Golf Club.

Where to Fish
Since the McKenzie has limited access, due to private property and a very difficult shoreline (to wade) it's our suggestion that you retain the services of a qualified McKenzie River guide. It's one of the better recreational investments you'll make.

Harry's Opinion
For sheer fishing pleasure, on one of the West's most notable streams, the McKenzie offers one of life's great rewards. But, as I said before, do it with a qualified guide.

Rating
The McKenzie River, with a guide, is a strong 7.

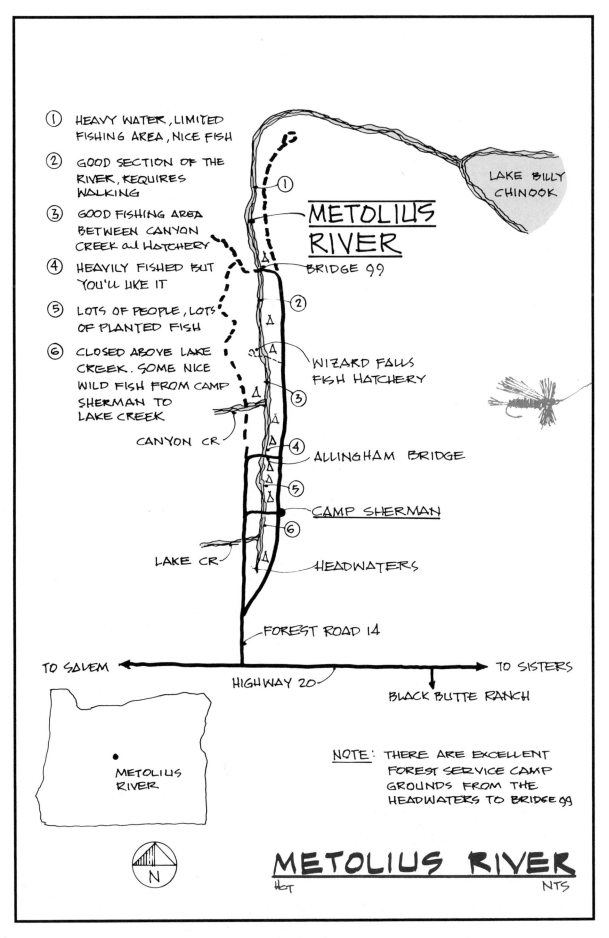

① HEAVY WATER, LIMITED FISHING AREA, NICE FISH

② GOOD SECTION OF THE RIVER, REQUIRES WALKING

③ GOOD FISHING AREA BETWEEN CANYON CREEK and HATCHERY

④ HEAVILY FISHED BUT YOU'LL LIKE IT

⑤ LOTS OF PEOPLE, LOTS OF PLANTED FISH

⑥ CLOSED ABOVE LAKE CREEK. SOME NICE WILD FISH FROM CAMP SHERMAN TO LAKE CREEK

CANYON CR

LAKE CR

METOLIUS RIVER

LAKE BILLY CHINOOK

BRIDGE 99

WIZARD FALLS FISH HATCHERY

ALLINGHAM BRIDGE

CAMP SHERMAN

HEADWATERS

FOREST ROAD 14

TO SALEM ← → TO SISTERS

HIGHWAY 20

BLACK BUTTE RANCH

METOLIUS RIVER

NOTE: THERE ARE EXCELLENT FOREST SERVICE CAMP GROUNDS FROM THE HEADWATERS TO BRIDGE 99

N

METOLIUS RIVER

HGT   NTS

The Metolius River

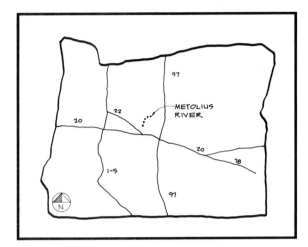

The Metolius, approximately 15 miles west of Sisters off Highway 20 flows through a beautiful setting of old-growth pine forests with spectacular mountain views. The camping facilities are excellent and help make this a wonderful family recreation area.

The headwaters of the Metolius offer one of the most beautiful scenes to be found in the Northwest. The river starts from springs near the base of Black Butte. At this site, the view across the mountain meadow and the river towards Mt. Jefferson is spectacular. See the suggestions on the accompanying map for some of the best places to fish the Metolius.

Type of Fish
Predominantly rainbows, some brown trout, whitefish and bull trout. General size is 8″ to 12″. Some get up to 3 to 5 pounds. Bull trout can get to 15 pounds, but average 3 to 5.

Equipment to Use
Rods: 1 to 7 weight.
Line: 6½′ to 9′.
Leaders: 5x and 6x, 9′ to 12′ (when dry). 7′ to 9′ with a strike indicator (when wet).
Reel: Palm drag.
Wading: Chest-high neoprenes and felt-soled, wading shoes.

Flies to Use
The Metolius has a wide variety of hatches throughout the year. Stones, caddis, mayflies, and midges, plus a number of terrestrials make up the diet of Metolius trout. In general, you'll find midges year around, mayflies and caddis from early spring to late fall, and stones in late spring and early summer.
Dry patterns: Comparadun, Green Drake, Adams, Golden Stone, Elk Hair Caddis, Salmon Flies, Flying Ant, Blue Dun and Renegade.
Nymphs: Girdle Bug, Kaufman Stone, Green Drake, Hares Ear, Sparkle Pupa and Pheasant Tail.
Bull trout: Use large streamers. For the best results, consult local fly shops concerning patterns.

When to Fish
The river seems to fish pretty well year around. You have to move up and down the river to find feeding fish, but they are there. Don't neglect winter fishing as there can be excellent action November through March. Another piece of advice: I've never found the Metolius to be an early morning stream. The best results seem to be after 9:30 AM.

Seasons & Limits
The river from Lake Creek to Bridge 99 is open year around (about 10 miles). Below Bridge 99, the trout season opens in late April. Since regulations change, you'll need to consult your ODFW synopsis before fishing. You can keep planted rainbows (clipped adipose fin) and whitefish, but all wild browns, rainbows and bull trout (adipose fin in place) must be returned to the water unharmed. The only exception is that you can keep Kokanee. The adipose fin *will* be in place. Again, because regulations change, consult the ODFW synopsis for the number and type of fish that can be kept.

Accommodations & Services
Very good lodging, restaurants, and stores at Camp Sherman, Black Butte Ranch and Sisters.

Harry's Opinion
The Metolius River is a fine fishing resource. However, it's tricky and it will take you some time to learn its idiosyncrasies, so be realistic with your expectations. It's a good stream for beginners and experts alike. Learn it, protect it and enjoy it. It's truly a gem by anyone's standards.

Rating
The Metolius is a strong 6.

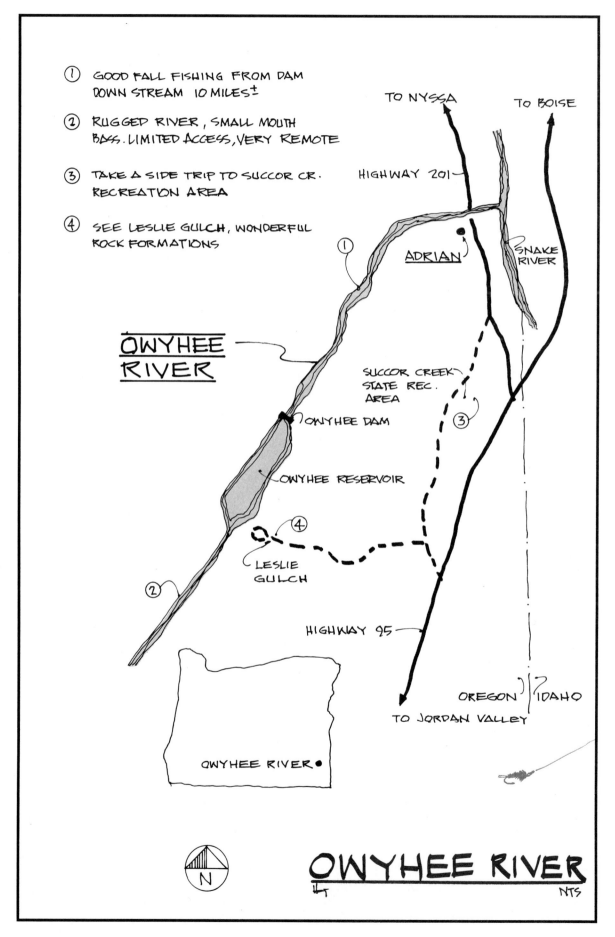

① GOOD FALL FISHING FROM DAM DOWN STREAM 10 MILES±

② RUGGED RIVER, SMALL MOUTH BASS. LIMITED ACCESS, VERY REMOTE

③ TAKE A SIDE TRIP TO SUCCOR CR. RECREATION AREA

④ SEE LESLIE GULCH, WONDERFUL ROCK FORMATIONS

TO NYSSA

TO BOISE

HIGHWAY 201

ADRIAN

SNAKE RIVER

OWYHEE RIVER

SUCCOR CREEK STATE REC. AREA

OWYHEE DAM

OWYHEE RESERVOIR

LESLIE GULCH

HIGHWAY 95

OREGON / IDAHO

TO JORDAN VALLEY

OWYHEE RIVER ●

N

OWYHEE RIVER

NTS

The Owyhee River

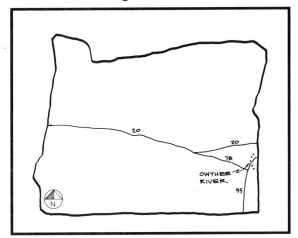

The Owyhee River runs easterly from its source in Nevada towards the town of Adrian and then flows into the Snake River. The only part of the Owyhee River I'll address here is that part of the river flowing from the Owyhee Dam downstream about 10 miles.

The geological formations along this river are fantastic. Rock formations and colors are stunning, to say the least. Even if you don't fish, the trip up the Owyhee River to the dam and Lake Owyhee is worth your time. In the fall, you can combine fishing with chukar hunting. You'll find plenty of both. The river is always off color (milky) but don't let that bother you. It's very fishable. See the suggestions on the accompanying map for some of the best places to fish the Owyhee.

Type of Fish
Rainbows from 7" to 15".

Equipment to Use
The Owyhee is a fairly good-sized river and long casts are sometimes needed.
Rods: 4 - 7 weight, 8' to 9'.
Line: Floating line to match rod weight.
Leaders: 4x and 5x, 9'.
Reel: Palm drag.
Wading: Waist-high or chest-high neoprenes and felt-soled wading shoes. Always carry a wading staff. It helps you probe the bottom in the off-colored water. Wade with care.

Flies to Use
There are hatches of midges and mayflies during the spring, summer and fall. My experience is that small patterns produce the best results.
Dry patterns: Adams, Comparadun, Pale Morning Dun, Black Spinner, Blue Dun and Renegade (#16 and #18).
Nymphs: Hares Ear, Midge Pupa, Pheasant Tail and Chironomid Pupa.

When to Fish
I like the fall, mid-September through October. The fish are active on the surface and are eager to attack most anything that is properly presented. Fishing is good all day long. It doesn't appear that one time is much better than another. I tend to favor the afternoon and evening fishing.

Season & Limits
The Owyhee below the dam is open year-round, but always consult the current ODFW synopsis because seasons and limits do change.

Accommodations & Services
There are a lot of good campsites along the river. Most are unimproved. Overnight accommodations, restaurants, gas and groceries are available in Adrain, Nyssa and at the resort on Lake Owyhee.

Harry's Opinion
The Owyhee River is a great place to spend time in the fall. The fishing can be very good. It's picturesque and there is plenty of sightseeing in the area. While you are there, you should take the drive through the Succor Creek State Recreational Area and Leslie Gulch. These two areas have exceptionally beautiful rock formations, canyons and other geologic features worth seeing.

Rating
The Owyhee rates a soft 5. Devoted Owyhee fly fishers won't agree with that low rating.

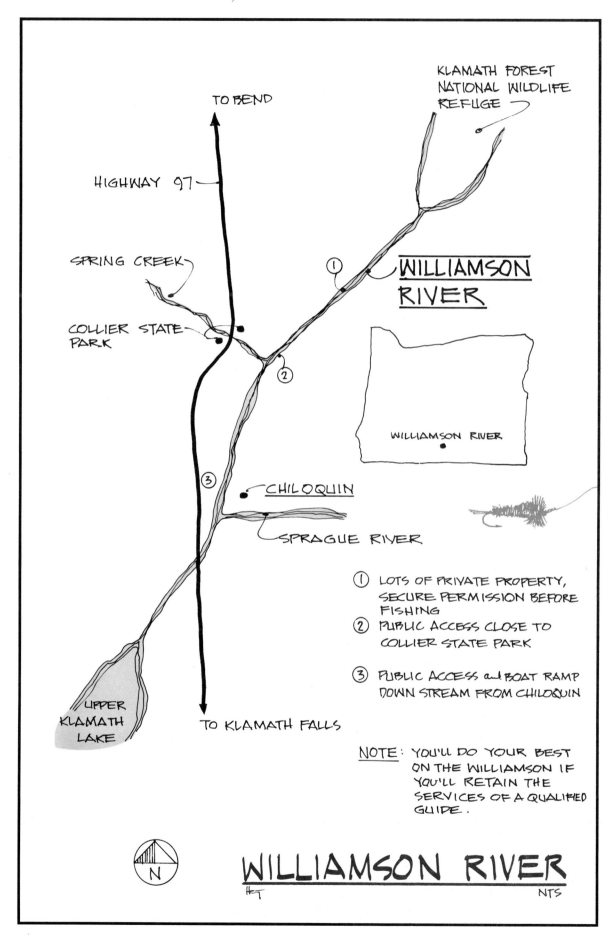

TO BEND

KLAMATH FOREST
NATIONAL WILDLIFE
REFUGE

HIGHWAY 97

SPRING CREEK

① WILLIAMSON
RIVER

COLLIER STATE
PARK

②

WILLIAMSON RIVER

③

CHILOQUIN

SPRAGUE RIVER

① LOTS OF PRIVATE PROPERTY,
SECURE PERMISSION BEFORE
FISHING
② PUBLIC ACCESS CLOSE TO
COLLIER STATE PARK

③ PUBLIC ACCESS and BOAT RAMP
DOWN STREAM FROM CHILOQUIN

UPPER
KLAMATH
LAKE

TO KLAMATH FALLS

NOTE: YOU'LL DO YOUR BEST
ON THE WILLIAMSON IF
YOU'LL RETAIN THE
SERVICES OF A QUALIFIED
GUIDE.

N

WILLIAMSON RIVER

HT   NTS

The Williamson River

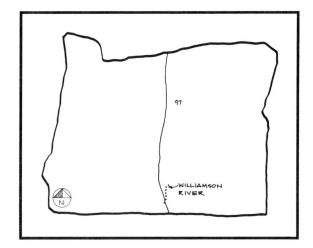

*T*he Williamson River is located north of Klamath Falls. It's crossed by Highway 97 near the town of Chiloquin.

I had a conversation one day with Polly Rosborough, the noted fly-tier and sportsman. He told me the Williamson River is the best, "big-fish" water in the country, and I think he's right. The big fish are not easy to catch, but on any given day you'll see more fish in the 5 to 10 pound range splashing around on the surface than you can reasonably imagine. If you want a chance to take big trout, hire a guide and head for the Williamson. If you aren't taking a guide, see the suggestions on the accompanying map for some of the best places to fish the Williamson.

Type of Fish
Large rainbow trout.

Equipment to Use
Rods: 6 - 9 weight, 8½' to 9½'.
Line: Floating and sink tip to match rod weight. Some guides like intermediate sink lines.
Leaders: 3x and 4x, plus a couple of 2x, just in case.
Reel: Mechanical and palm drag.
Wading: Neoprene waders with felt-soled wading shoes. I'd also take a wading staff.

Flies to Use
There are heavy mayfly and caddis hatches on the Williamson. These hatches seem to be at their best in June and July.
Dry patterns: Elk Hair Caddis, Comparadun, Adams, Humpy, Irresistible and Pale Morning Dun.
Nymphs & streamers: Maribou Leech, Matuka, Wooly Bugger, Muddler Minnow, and Zonker.

When to Fish
June through October is when the big fish move up from Upper Klamath Lake. A guide indicated that the time of day wasn't as important as your success at putting the fly in the right place. Frankly, if you haven't fished the Williamson before, you'll save a lot of learning time and effort by hiring a qualified guide.

Season & Limits
The fishing opens in late May and closes the end of October. There are varying regulations on the Williamson, so refer to the ODFW synopsis before fishing.

Accommodations & Services
There are good camping facilities at Spring Creek and a motel, restaurants, and a service station near Chiloquin.

Harry's Opinion
The Williamson River is a unique fishery. As mentioned before, if you want the best opportunity to catch big trout in an Oregon stream, head to the Williamson.

Rating
The Williamson is an 8 for big fish opportunity.

Comments on
Other Rivers and Creeks

Little Blitzen

The Little Blitzen is a tributary of the Blitzen (Donner and Blitzen) and flows into the Blitzen about three miles down from Blitzen Crossing. Blitzen Crossing is located on the Steens Mountain Loop Road. The Little Blitzen can be accessed through the Clemens Ranch, which has been deeded to the BLM. For specific information, consult BLM personnel at their office on Highway 20 just west of Hines. The Little Blitzen is fly fishing only and catch and release.

Big Indian and Little Indian Creeks

These two creeks are on the west side of the Steens Mountain and can be accessed off the Steens Mountain Loop Road. These are small streams and they hold a good population of native rainbows. They can't stand much pressure, so please practice catch and release when you fish the creeks. Plan on doing lots of walking. The terrain along these creeks will amaze you. It's really something else.

Other Streams in the Steens Mountains

You'll find numerous small streams cascading down the Steens Mountain. Names like Kiger Creek, McCoy Creek, Ankle Creek, Wild Horse Creek and Skull Creek all hold wild fish. To access some of these, you must cross private land, and that can pose a problem. Contact the BLM staff (on Highway 20 west of Hines) for some guidance.

North Fork of the Malheur River

The section above Beulah Reservoir that is accessible only by foot can provide some exceptional rainbow fishing. Study a good topographical map and select a likely spot. It's my guess you'll be glad you gave the North Fork a try.

Deep Creek

Deep Creek is located southeast of Lakeview and parallels Highway 140. It's a good fly fishing stream with both stocked and wild fish available. Information on Deep Creek can be obtained from the ODFW regional office in Hines.

Crescent Creek

It's hardly a household word in Central Oregon, but it is a nice fly fishing stream. The creek has plenty of access and a good population of brown and rainbow trout. Dexters Fly Shop in La Pine or the ODFW office in Bend should be able to assist you with information on Crescent Creek. Crescent Creek can be accessed off Highway 58 west of Highway 97.

Little Deschutes River

This meandering stream crosses Highway 58 east of where Crescent Creek crosses the highway. It has some good-sized brown trout and rainbows. If you are in a mood for exploring new trout water, you just might want to give the Little Deschutes a try.

Notes

Notes

Section II

Some Thoughts on Fishing and Selected Lakes and Reservoirs

*F*ishing lakes and reservoirs is a whole different program than fishing streams. On streams, it's relatively easy to read the water and determine the feeding lanes and holds. That's not true with the still water of lakes. The surface is flat without a lot of indicators to tell you where to fish. Look at the shore line, identify submerged objects, study contour maps of the bottom, scan for surface activity and observe where other people are fishing. You may need to keep moving and exploring until you find where the fish are active. This active spot can change from hour to hour.

To give you an example of what I'm talking about, I once had a banner day fishing Davis Lake (page 35). I fished the main lake, near the O'Dell Creek channel, with a small Adams pattern. (Fishing dry flies for Davis fish always excites me.) Two days later I took my son Brad to this hot spot.

There were about eight other boats in the vicinity which seemed to indicate that the fish were still working the area. We anchored and started fishing, while observing what kind of success other people were having. After about 45 minutes we hadn't a rise and saw only one other fish taken. I switched to a nymph with the same results: nothing. About this time, we noted several fish working the reed beds almost into the channel. We pulled anchor and headed towards the rising fish. We positioned the boat, anchored, switched to dry patterns and started casting towards the reeds. The first cast produced a rise, but no fish.

That was the last fish we'd see coming to a dry pattern. We didn't do anything on Montanas or Leeches either. We then moved well into the channel just before calling it a day.

On the way in I put on a Prince nymph and cast towards the reeds. After several casts I hooked a nice fish. We anchored. Over the next hour we enjoyed catching and releasing a dozen Rainbows from 13″ to 20″. This was just a case of observing, moving, changing patterns and plain old fisherman's luck .

The message I convey is: don't get too enamored with what happened yesterday or that morning, but concentrate on finding the fish when you're on the water. There are times when you'll need all your skill and luck to accomplish this.

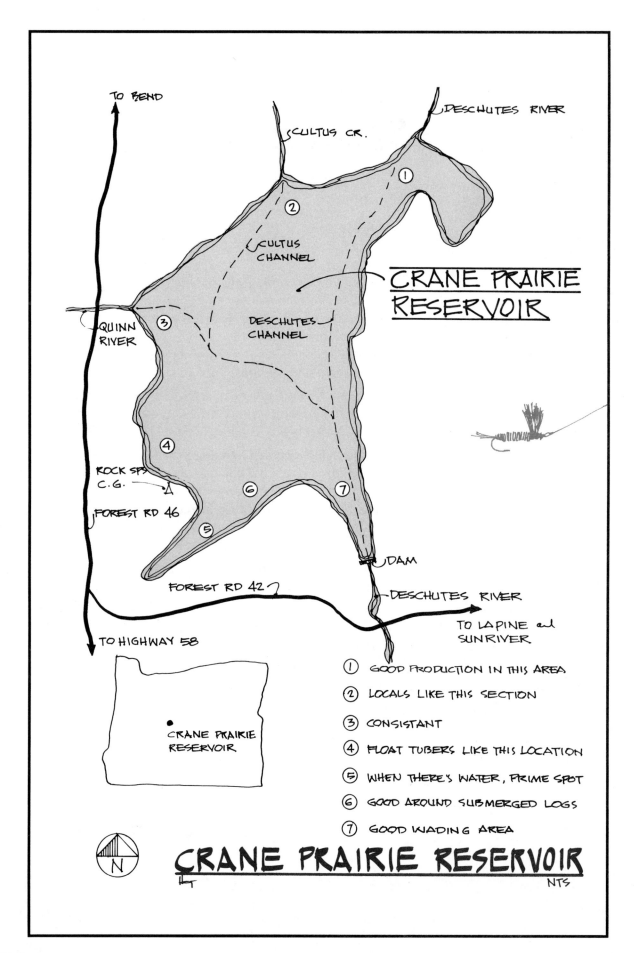

TO BEND

DESCHUTES RIVER

CULTUS CR.

①

②

CULTUS CHANNEL

CRANE PRAIRIE RESERVOIR

DESCHUTES CHANNEL

QUINN RIVER

③

④

ROCK SPS C.G.

FOREST RD 46

⑥

⑦

⑤

FOREST RD 42

DAM

DESCHUTES RIVER

TO LAPINE and SUNRIVER

TO HIGHWAY 58

CRANE PRAIRIE RESERVOIR

① GOOD PRODUCTION IN THIS AREA

② LOCALS LIKE THIS SECTION

③ CONSISTANT

④ FLOAT TUBERS LIKE THIS LOCATION

⑤ WHEN THERE'S WATER, PRIME SPOT

⑥ GOOD AROUND SUBMERGED LOGS

⑦ GOOD WADING AREA

N

CRANE PRAIRIE RESERVOIR

NTS

Crane Prairie Reservoir

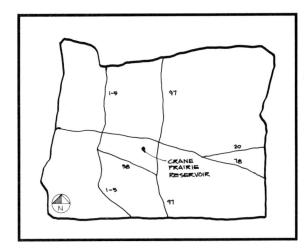

rane Prairie Reservoir lies west of Bend and can be accessed from Century Drive (Forest Highway 46) or Forest Highway 42 from Sunriver.

This is one of the finest fly fishing reservoirs in the West. It has more than its share of big trout, scenery and wildlife viewing opportunities. See the suggestions on the accompanying map for some of the best places to fish Crane Prairie Reservoir.

Type of Fish
You'll find rainbow and brook trout with a fair population of kokanee and bass. The size of the trout are amazing: 3 to 5 pound fish are common, and fish in the 10 pound range are recorded annually.

Equipment to Use
This is BIG trout water so you'll need equipment that can handle large fish.
Rods: 6 and 7 weight.
Line: Matching floating or sink tip.
Leaders: 3x, 4x and 5x, 9' to 12'.
Reel: Mechanical and palm drag.
Wading: For the most part, you'll find fishing from a floating device most productive. But, there are some places where wading can be very rewarding. Chest high waders and wading shoes are desirable at Crane Prairie.

Flies to Use
Crane has a real smorgasbord of aquatic food for the trout. Damsel flies, dragon flies, mayflies, scuds and leeches make up a portion of the buffet.
Dry patterns: Comparadun, Adams, Mayflies, Callibaetis, Spinner and Pale Morning Dun.
Nymphs: Prince, Scuds, Montana, Leech, Damsel and Hares Ear and maybe even a Crane Prairie Special.

When to Fish
Crane Prairie is one of those places you can experience good fishing any time during the season.

Season & Limits
The season opens in late April and closes the end of October. For exact dates and limit regulations, refer to the ODFW Synopsis.

Accommodations & Services
Crane Prairie is blessed with good camping facilities. There is a store, food service and gas available at the resort at Gails Landing. In the vicinity, there is Twin Lakes Resort and complete services at Sunriver, La Pine and Bend.

Harry's Opinion
If you only have time to fish one place on your trip to Central Oregon and want the opportunity to catch trophy fish, test your skills at Crane Prairie Reservoir.

Rating
An 8.5.

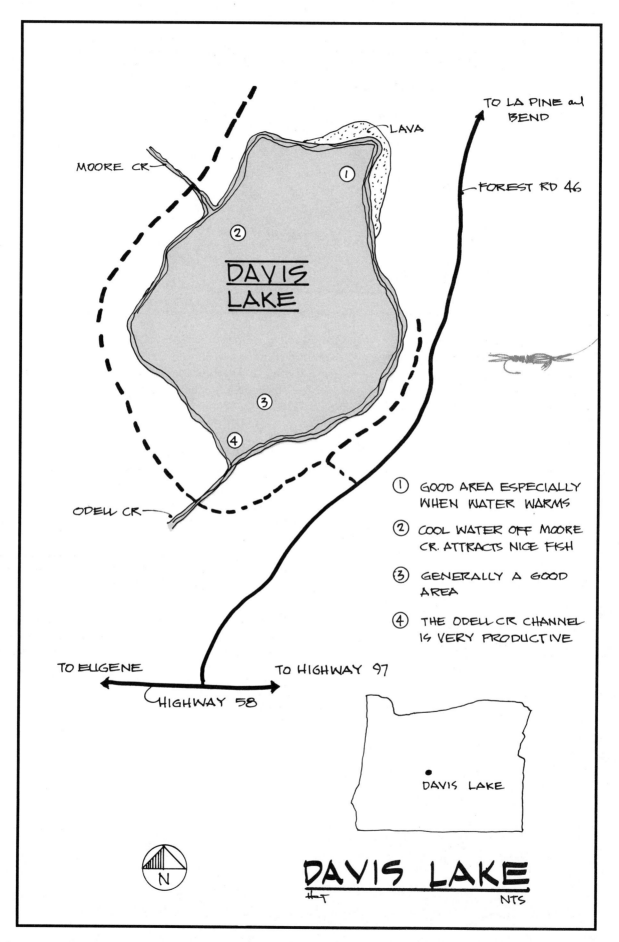

MOORE CR

LAVA

TO LA PINE and BEND

FOREST RD 46

①

②

DAVIS LAKE

③

④

ODELL CR

① GOOD AREA ESPECIALLY WHEN WATER WARMS

② COOL WATER OFF MOORE CR. ATTRACTS NICE FISH

③ GENERALLY A GOOD AREA

④ THE ODELL CR CHANNEL IS VERY PRODUCTIVE

TO EUGENE

TO HIGHWAY 97

HIGHWAY 58

DAVIS LAKE

N

DAVIS LAKE

NTS

Davis Lake

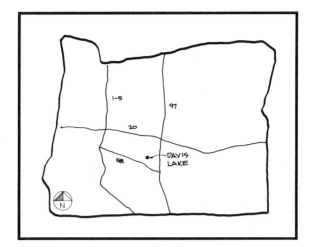

avis Lake is located in both Deschutes and Klamath Counties. It can be accessed off Forest Route 46, west of La Pine.

During the recent drought period in Central Oregon, Davis Lake experienced low water conditions and relatively poor fishing. When water conditions improve, it won't take long for the lake to return to its glory days. When Davis is right, it's one fine fishery. See the suggestions on the accompanying map for some of the best places to fish Davis Lake.

Type of Fish
Primarily rainbow trout; however, other species have been introduced by ODFW. When Davis is at its best, 2 to 5 pound trout are common.

Equipment to Use
Rods: 5, 6 and 7 weight.
Line: Floating and sink tip to match rod weight.
Leaders: 4x and 5x, 9'.
Reel: Mechanical and palm drag.
Wading: You can wade some portions of the lake. Best you have chest-high neoprenes with wading boots. Davis is a good float-tubing lake, especially around the O'Dell Creek channel. Boats (type and design of your choice) are in order. There are launching sites at the camp grounds.

Flies to Use
Davis is rich with aquatic life. There are extensive hatches of midges, mayflies and mosquitoes. Nymphing is generally the best technique.
Dry patterns: Adams, Comparadun, Pale Morning Dun and Callibaetis.
Nymphs: Damsel, Prince, Zug Bug, Montana and Leech.

When to Fish
Good fishing, when the water conditions are right, is available throughout the season. I feel the best time is late May or June and again in late September and October. My experience is that it fishes well all day long.

Season & Limits
The season opens in late April and closes the end of October. Before fishing, review the ODFW synopsis for exact dates and limit regulations.

Accommodations & Services
There are excellent campgrounds at Davis, but for most other services you'll have to drive to La Pine, Sunriver or Bend. There are resorts at South Twin Lake and Crane Prairie that have restaurants, groceries and gas.

Harry's Opinion
The water conditions at Davis were not favorable in the late 80's and early 90's. Fishing was relatively poor. However, Davis has an abundance of food for growing big trout and a good water year(s), along with the introduction of a different strain of rainbow trout, should bring Davis back as one of the prime lakes in Oregon.

Rating
Davis, as of this writing, was a soft 2. With proper water conditions and time it will be a 9.

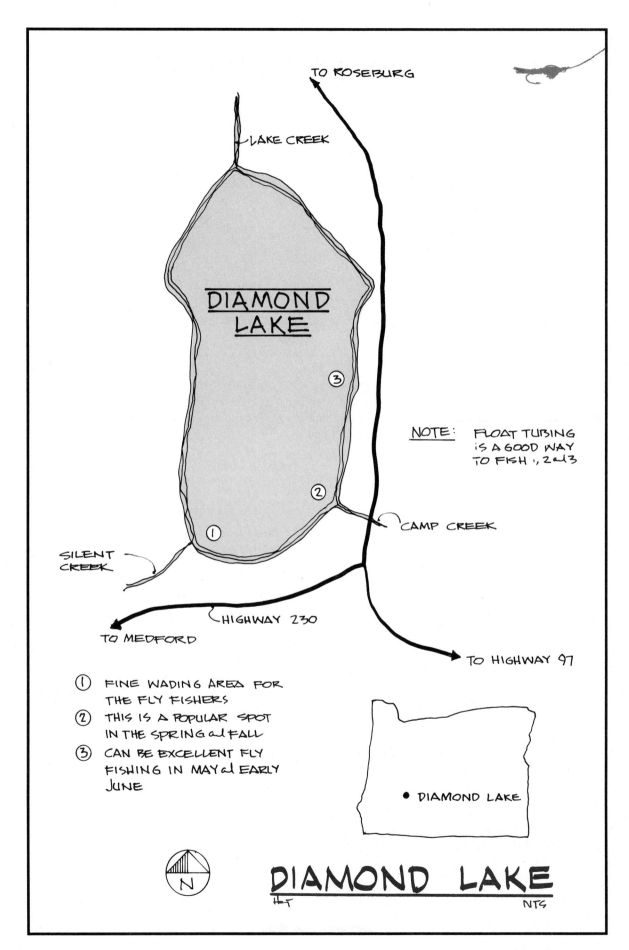

TO ROSEBURG

LAKE CREEK

DIAMOND
LAKE

③

NOTE: FLOAT TUBING
IS A GOOD WAY
TO FISH 1, 2 and 3

②

CAMP CREEK

①

SILENT
CREEK

HIGHWAY 230

TO MEDFORD

TO HIGHWAY 97

① FINE WADING AREA FOR
THE FLY FISHERS
② THIS IS A POPULAR SPOT
IN THE SPRING and FALL
③ CAN BE EXCELLENT FLY
FISHING IN MAY and EARLY
JUNE

● DIAMOND LAKE

N

DIAMOND LAKE

HT

NTS

Diamond Lake

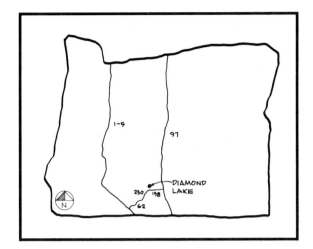

Diamond Lake is located in Douglas County and is accessed by Highway 138. It can be approached from the east from Highway 97 via Highway 138 and from the south and west on Highways 230 and 138.

This may be the most productive lake in the state. People tend to think of it as a trolling and bait-fishing lake, and it is, but you can also have great fly fishing action. See the suggestions on the accompanying map for some of the best places to fish Diamond Lake.

Diamond Lake offers a wonderful mountain setting. To the west is Mt. Bailey and to the east sits Mt. Thielsen. The lake rests in a heavily forested area. It's just a short drive from Diamond to Crater Lake National Park, a "must see" while in Oregon.

Type of Fish
Rainbow trout from 10″ to 24″ with most averaging over a pound. A good number of fish over 5 pounds are taken each year.

Equipment to Use
Rods: 6 or 7 weight, 9′ to 9½′.
Line: Floating line to match rod size.
Leaders: 4x or 5x and 9′.
Reel: Mechanical and palm drag.
Wading: The lake can be fished from boats, float-tubes or by wading. You'll need chest-high waders and boots for float-tubing and wading. I like neoprene waders best.

Flies to Use
There are some fine hatches at Diamond Lake, especially midges and mayflies in the spring.
Dry patterns: Midge, Comparadun, Adams and Blue Dun.
Nymphs: Leech, Damsel, Hares Ear and Chironomids.

When to Fish
When the ice first thaws, and the fish start their spring spawning, you'll find some exceptional fly fishing. This occurs about the time the season opens in late April and remains good through May and sometimes early June. Fly fishing picks up again in the fall months of September and October. The lake fishes well nearly all day long.

Season & Limits
The season opens in late April and continues through the end of October. There has been a 10 fish per day limit; however, for exact dates and limits, consult the current ODFW synopsis.

Accommodations & Services
There are good campgrounds along the lake. Accommodations, food service, stores and gas are available at Diamond Lake Lodge. Boat launching ramps are located in several places around the lake.

Harry's Opinion
This is one of the finest lake fisheries in the West. If you want an opportunity to catch plenty of quality trout, put Diamond Lake on your list of places to go.

Rating
Diamond Lake, in terms of all types of fishing is a 9. For fly fishing, it's a 7.5.

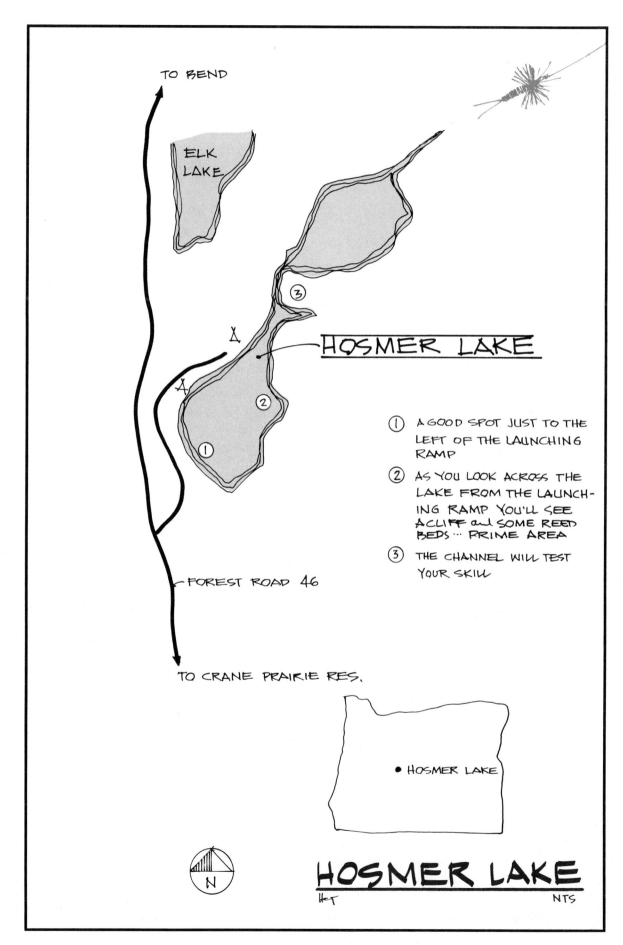

TO BEND

ELK
LAKE

③

HOSMER LAKE

① A GOOD SPOT JUST TO THE
LEFT OF THE LAUNCHING
RAMP

② AS YOU LOOK ACROSS THE
LAKE FROM THE LAUNCH-
ING RAMP YOU'LL SEE
A CLIFF and SOME REED
BEDS ··· PRIME AREA

③ THE CHANNEL WILL TEST
YOUR SKILL

②

①

FOREST ROAD 46

TO CRANE PRAIRIE RES.

• HOSMER LAKE

N

HOSMER LAKE
HcT   NTS

Hosmer Lake

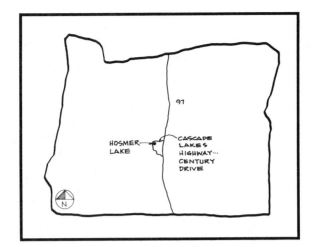

Hosmer Lake is located in Deschutes County, about 35 miles west of Bend. It is accessed off Century Drive (Forest Highway 46).

One of the most unique fly-fishing only fisheries in the state of Oregon, it's a relatively shallow lake with a rich food supply. It's a real favorite of Central Oregon fly fishers because of the Atlantic Salmon. See the suggestions on the accompanying map for some of the best places to fish Hosmer Lake.

Type of Fish
Good quality Atlantic salmon and brook trout. Both species grow to nice size in this food-rich environment.

Equipment to Use
Rods: 4 to 7 weight, 8½' to 9½'.
Line: Floating lines, matched to the weight of the rod are most popular. Sink tip lines are used at times.
Leaders: 4x and 5x, 9' to 15'.
Reel: Mechanical and palm drag.
Wading: To fish Hosmer properly, you'll need either a boat, canoe or float tube. There are restrictions on motor use, so be sure to consult the ODFW synopsis. If you're going to use a float tube, bring chest-high, neoprene waders, wading shoes and fins.

Flies to Use
There are good hatches at Hosmer through most of the season.
Dry patterns: Adams, Comparadun, Water Boatman, Caddis and Callibaetis.
Nymphs: Leech, Stovepipe, Damsel, Scuds, Cates Turkey and Timberline Emerger.

When to Fish
It's a mixed bag of opinions. Some like June-July, while others prefer late September. I feel both are good times, with good opportunities to take nice size fish. Most all Hosmer fly fishers agree that evening is the best time of the day for any kind of fly fishing.

Season & Limits
The season opens in late April and continues through the end of October. For exact dates and limits, consult the current ODFW synopsis.

Accommodations & Services
There are good campgrounds at the lake. The nearest accommodations, food and gas are located at Elk Lake Resort, just a few miles away. A full range of services are available in Bend.

Harry's Opinion
Hosmer is a very scenic lake with lots of wildlife. If you're looking for a lake that will challenge your fly fishing skills, don't look any farther, just head for Hosmer.

Rating
A 5.5.

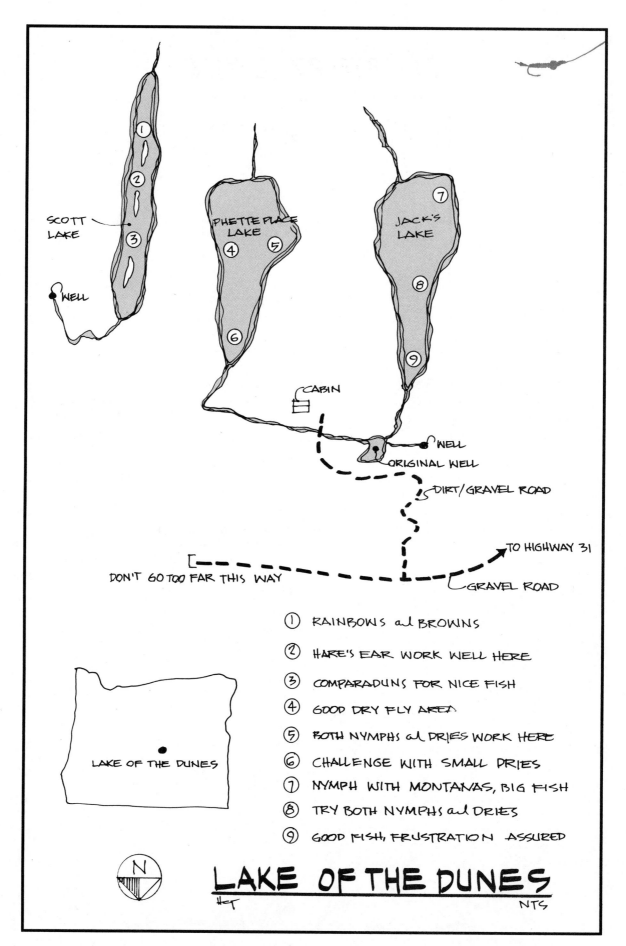

SCOTT LAKE

WELL

PHETTE PLACE LAKE

JACK'S LAKE

CABIN

WELL

ORIGINAL WELL

DIRT/GRAVEL ROAD

TO HIGHWAY 31

DON'T GO TOO FAR THIS WAY

GRAVEL ROAD

① RAINBOWS and BROWNS

② HARE'S EAR WORK WELL HERE

③ COMPARADUNS FOR NICE FISH

④ GOOD DRY FLY AREA

⑤ BOTH NYMPHS and DRIES WORK HERE

⑥ CHALLENGE WITH SMALL DRIES

⑦ NYMPH WITH MONTANAS, BIG FISH

⑧ TRY BOTH NYMPHS and DRIES

⑨ GOOD FISH, FRUSTRATION ASSURED

LAKE OF THE DUNES

N

LAKE OF THE DUNES

HcT

NTS

Lake of the Dunes (private)

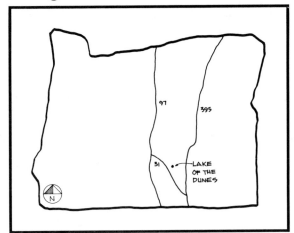

The Lake of the Dunes is located near Summer Lake off Highway 31. It's about 75 miles southeast of La Pine.

The Lake really should be called *Lakes* of the Dunes because there are actually three small desert lakes at the site. These lakes are fed by artesian wells which provide a constant flow of 55° water. Most importantly, the lakes are a challenge to fish. And they grow BIG fish. The cost for this private fishery is modest compared to most, and is the best pay-to-fish bargain I know of in the region. See the suggestions on the accompanying map for some of the best places to fish Lake of the Dunes.

Type of Fish
Predominantly rainbows, but Montana browns have been introduced and are doing well. The average fish is 12″ to 15″ with Rainbows from 3 to 6 pounds. The record fish was close to 16 pounds.

Equipment to Use
Rods: 3 to 7 weight, 8½′ to 9½′. Rod weight depends on weather and wind. There can be heavy winds on the desert, especially in the spring months.
Line: Floating line matched to rod weight.
Leaders: 4x, 5x and 6x, 9′ to 12′.
Reel: Mechanical and palm drag.
Wading: Chest-high waders with felt-soled wading shoes or even hip boots. A float tube will probably put fish down. Better to wade.

Flies to Use
The fly selection on the lakes is fairly simple, but your presentation will have a great deal to do with your success.
Dry patterns: Comparadun, Adams, Elk Hair Caddis, Olive Dun, and Callibaetis.
Nymphs: Prince, Damsel, Chironomid, Hares Ear, Montana, Wooly Bugger and Pheasant Tail.

When to Fish
Lake of the Dunes is fairly consistent from March until the end of October. It fishes well all day long, but I think it's best from, say 8:00 AM until about 1:00 PM. I've got some fishing pals that don't agree with me. They like early morning.

Season & Limits
The season is from the first of March until the end of October. It is catch-and-release only, with barbless hooks.

Accommodations & Services
There is a rustic log cabin on site that will accommodate 5 people. It comes with a kitchen, cooking utensils, refrigerator and, most important, a bath with a shower. There's a motel in Summer Lake, about seven miles from the Lake of the Dunes. There's also a gas station, a restaurant and country store.

Harry's Opinion
Fishing the Lakes is no gimmee. It takes a reasonable level of skill. If you like remoteness, desert country, challenge, good fishing and the sound of silence, this is your type of place. By the way, when you're on the property, you are the only party allowed to fish during your reservation.

Rating
The "Lakes" are a solid 8.

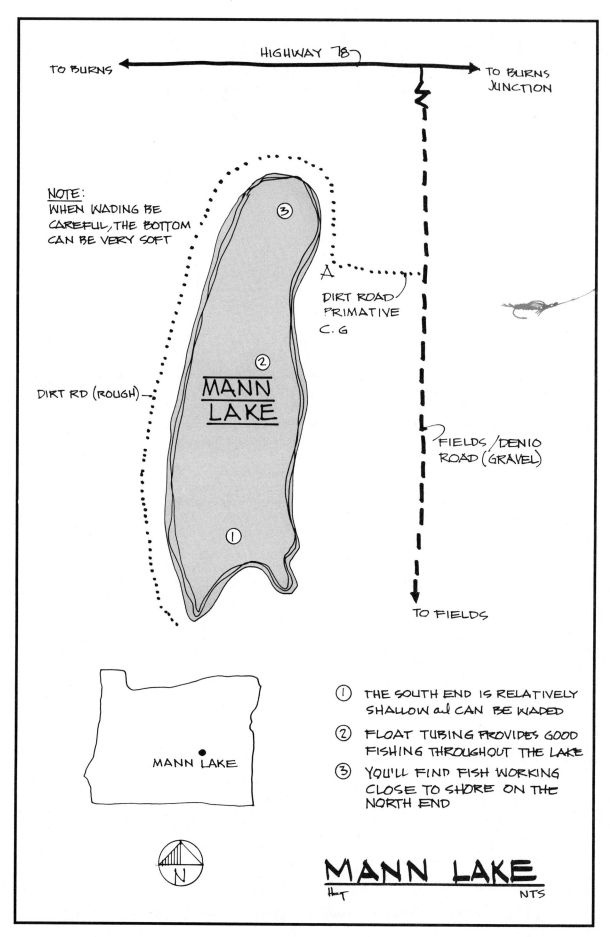

HIGHWAY 78

TO BURNS

TO BURNS JUNCTION

NOTE:
WHEN WADING BE CAREFUL, THE BOTTOM CAN BE VERY SOFT

③

A
DIRT ROAD
PRIMATIVE
C. G

② MANN LAKE

DIRT RD (ROUGH)

FIELDS/DENIO ROAD (GRAVEL)

①

TO FIELDS

MANN LAKE

① THE SOUTH END IS RELATIVELY SHALLOW and CAN BE WADED

② FLOAT TUBING PROVIDES GOOD FISHING THROUGHOUT THE LAKE

③ YOU'LL FIND FISH WORKING CLOSE TO SHORE ON THE NORTH END

N

MANN LAKE

HT   NTS

Mann Lake

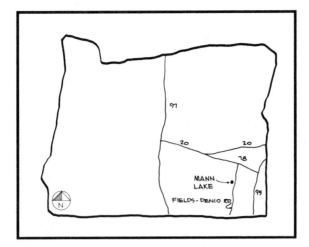

*M*ann Lake lies on the east side of the Steens Mountain. Take Highway 78 out of Burns and turn south on the Fields-Denio Road (some maps call it Folly Farm Road). This is a good gravel road. From the turnoff on Highway 78 its about 35 miles to Mann Lake. Mann Lake is remote and if there is such a thing as a pure desert lake, this is it. With the Steens Mountain as a backdrop, and the desert floor as a stage, Mann Lake will dazzle you with exceptional desert scenery and good size fish. See the suggestions on the accompanying map for some of the best places to fish Mann Lake.

Type of Fish
Cutthroat that run from 12″ to 20″, with some a little larger.

Equipment to Use
Rods: 4 to 7 weight depending on the weather.
Line: Floating line to match rod weight.
Leaders: 3x, 4x and 5x, 9′.
Reel: Palm and mechanical drag.
Wading: It is possible to get to fish by wading the lake, but it's hard. Mann Lake's bottom is very soft and in some areas you're in muck up to your knees. The best way to fish Mann is from a float tube; the choice of most experienced Mann Lake fly fishers. Boats and canoes are also used.

Flies to Use
You'll have the best results on Mann Lake using nymphs and streamers: Zug Bug, Wooly Bugger, Leech, Damsel, Prince and Zonker. Fishing on the lake is restricted to barbless flies and lures.

When to Fish
As soon as the ice is off the lake in the spring, things start to happen. This action continues until the water warms in July and August. Good fishing starts again in late September and October. The time of day doesn't seem to make that much difference.

Season & Limits
Mann Lake is open year around. All fish under 16″ must be returned to the lake unharmed. The limit is 2 fish over 16″. Since regulations are subject to change, refer to the ODFW synopsis for current regulations.

Accommodations & Services
This is very simple: there are not any accommodations or services within 50 miles of the lake. The campground on the north end of the lake is unimproved and drinking water is not available. If you need something, you'll have to travel about 50 miles south to Fields (they have great hamburgers at Fields) or the Princeton/Crane area or return to Burns. The gravel roads in this area are well maintained but have a reputation as tire eaters. Several years ago, I had two blowouts in 35 miles. That takes a lot of fun out of the day. Be sure your gas tank and water containers are full before departing for Mann Lake.

Harry's Opinion
If you haven't experienced fly fishing a true desert lake, you should try Mann. It's roughly 270 acres in size (may vary with precipitation) which is large enough for elbow room. In the spring and fall, Mann Lake is an exceptional fishery. Word of warning: wind. There are times when the wind can prevent fly fishing. It forces you to park your car on top of your tent to keep it from blowing into Idaho.

Rating
A very solid 6.5.

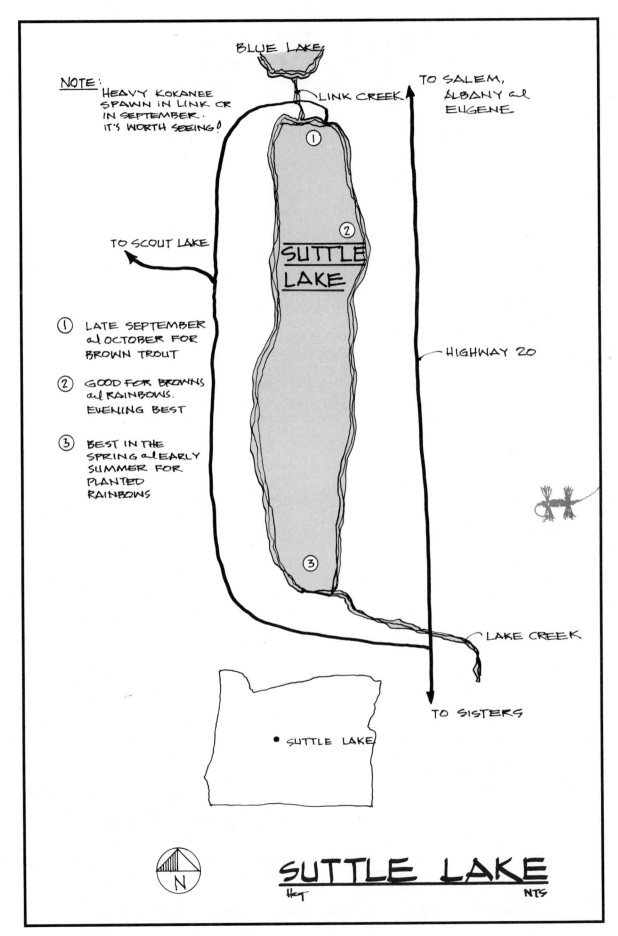

BLUE LAKE

NOTE: HEAVY KOKANEE SPAWN IN LINK CR IN SEPTEMBER. IT'S WORTH SEEING!

LINK CREEK

TO SALEM, ALBANY and EUGENE

①

②

SUTTLE LAKE

TO SCOUT LAKE

HIGHWAY 20

① LATE SEPTEMBER and OCTOBER FOR BROWN TROUT

② GOOD FOR BROWNS and RAINBOWS. EVENING BEST

③ BEST IN THE SPRING and EARLY SUMMER FOR PLANTED RAINBOWS

③

LAKE CREEK

TO SISTERS

• SUTTLE LAKE

N

SUTTLE LAKE

Heg

NTS

❖ 44 ❖

Suttle Lake

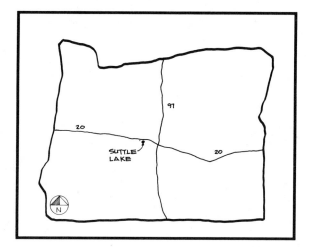

his large lake is about 15 miles west of Sisters on the south side of Highway 20. The lake is surrounded by pine forest and there are some excellent views of the nearby Cascade Mountains. When a lake is this easy to get to, you wouldn't expect it to have a good population of large brown trout. Suttle has them, nonetheless, and they can be taken with flies. Suttle Lake is one of the better family lakes in the region with excellent campgrounds and boat launching ramps. There are a lot of recreational activities available around Suttle Lake; horseback riding, hiking and water skiing to name a few. See the suggestions on the accompanying map for some of the best places to fish Suttle Lake.

Type of Fish
You'll find brown and rainbow trout and a strong population of kokanee (landlocked salmon). Browns will be from 1 to 5 pounds. A few are bigger. Rainbows are planted and average from 8″ to 12″. Kokanee will be in the 9″ to 14″ range.

Equipment to Use
Rods: 5, 6 or 7 weight, 8½′ to 9½′.
Line: Floating and sink tip for flexibility.
Leaders: 3x, 4x and 5x, 9′.
Reel: Mechanical and palm drag.
Wading: Chest-high, neoprene waders and felt-soled wading boots. Float tubing is a good method of fishing Suttle. You'll need the same wading equipment for tubing, along with a pair of fins. Most people fish Suttle Lake from boats.

Flies to Use
As you would expect, fly patterns will change depending on the time of year you're fishing Suttle. Ask around.
Dry patterns: Renegade, Adams, Royal Wulff, Comparadun.
Nymphs and Streamers: Hares Ear, Prince, Carey Special, Zonker, Muddler, Wooly Bugger.

When to Fish
You'll find the best fishing in May and June and again in late September and October. For browns, it's best late in the year, with late afternoon and evening being most productive. Generally, there aren't any water skiers during these time periods.

Season & Limits
Suttle opens in late April and closes the end of October. Limits vary and are subject to change, so consult the ODFW synopsis for exact dates and bag limits.

Accommodations & Services
There are campgrounds on the south side and the west end of the lake. A store and restaurant are located on the west end and a store and small dock sit on the east end of the lake. There are overnight accommodations available at Blue Lake, in Sisters, Camp Sherman and Black Butte Ranch. Restaurants, gas and groceries are available in Camp Sherman and Sisters. Other restaurants and a store are located at Black Butte Ranch.

Harry's Opinion
If you're looking for an easy access lake with better than average fishing, Suttle is a good choice. It may be the most underrated lake in Central Oregon.

Rating
Suttle, for overall fishing is a 6.5. For fly fishing it's a soft 5.

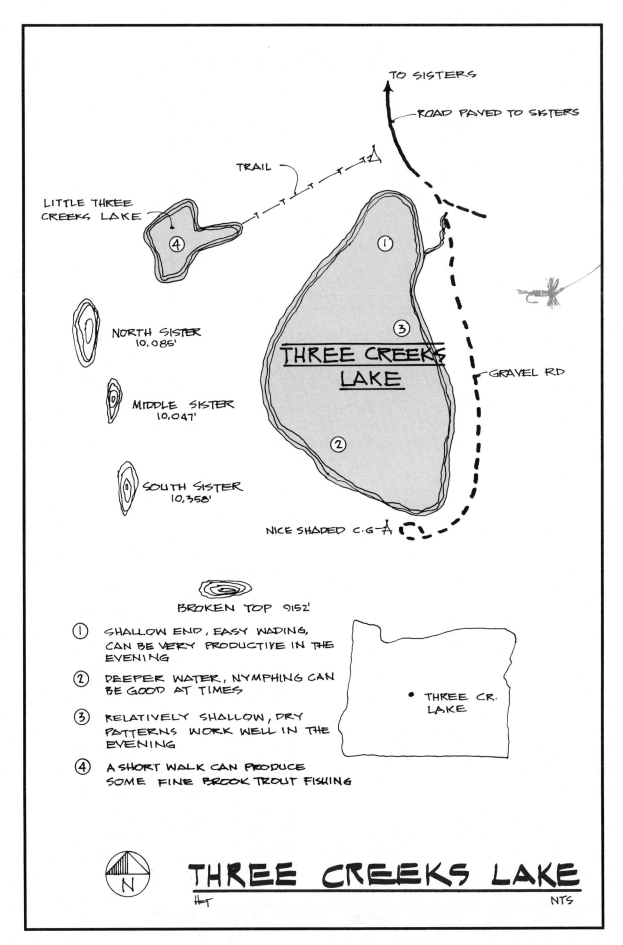

TO SISTERS

ROAD PAVED TO SISTERS

TRAIL

LITTLE THREE
CREEKS LAKE

④

① THREE CREEKS LAKE

③

GRAVEL RD

NORTH SISTER
10,085'

MIDDLE SISTER
10,047'

②

SOUTH SISTER
10,358'

NICE SHADED C.G ⚓

BROKEN TOP 9152'

① SHALLOW END, EASY WADING,
CAN BE VERY PRODUCTIVE IN THE
EVENING

② DEEPER WATER, NYMPHING CAN
BE GOOD AT TIMES

③ RELATIVELY SHALLOW, DRY
PATTERNS WORK WELL IN THE
EVENING

④ A SHORT WALK CAN PRODUCE
SOME FINE BROOK TROUT FISHING

• THREE CR.
LAKE

THREE CREEKS LAKE

HT

NTS

Three Creeks Lake

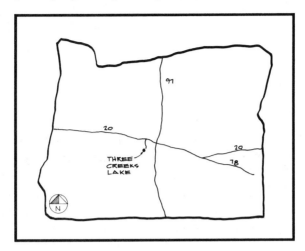

hree Creeks Lake is 18 miles south of Sisters at the base of Broken Top and the Three Sisters Mountains. The lake and its smaller cousin, Little Three Creeks Lake, are in a beautiful high Cascade, alpine setting at approximately 6,500'. Here is a fishing trip that's worth the ride for the scenic value alone. Besides the scenery, odds are in your favor that you'll catch some fish. See the suggestions on the accompanying map for some of the best places to fish Three Creeks Lake.

Type of Fish
Three Creeks Lake has both rainbow and brook trout that run from 8" to 15". Little Three Creeks Lake has a good population of brook trout that will go to about 14".

Equipment to Use
Rods: 3 to 7 weight.
Line: Floating line to match rod weight. Some fly fishers like to use sink tip line, though I haven't found it that necessary.
Leaders: 4x and 5x leaders, 9'.
Reel: Palm drag is adequate.
Wading: There are parts of the lake you can wade. You'll need chest-high waders and wading boots. Float tubing is a good way to fish the lake. If you prefer a boat, that's OK too. Motors are *NOT* allowed on Three Creeks, or Little Three Creeks Lakes. Float tube enthusiasts should note that to get to Little Three Creeks Lake requires about a mile hike.

Flies to Use
Dry patterns: Adams, Renegade, Elk Hair Caddis, Comparadun, Ant and Royal Wulff.
Nymphs: Hares Ear, Polly Casual Dress, Pheasant Tail, and Chironomid.

When to Fish
July, August, September and October are regarded as the best months. The evening hours produce the best fly fishing.

Season & Limits
The season opens in late April and closes the end of October. For limits and exact dates, refer to the ODFW synopsis.

Accommodations & Services
There are several very nice campgrounds and a seasonal store with boat rentals at the lake. All other services are available in Sisters.

Harry's Opinion
Three Creeks and Little Three Creeks Lake are fun to fish. To get to Little Three Creeks Lake requires about a half an hour hike from the Driftwood camp ground. Just going up to Three Creeks Lake is well worth the trip.

Rating
Three Creeks and Little Three Creeks are soft 5's.

Comments on
Other Lakes and Reservoirs

Ana Reservoir

As the source of the Ana River, this small reservoir is ice free most of the year. It's fed by springs with water temperatures of around 56°. I've had some good days fly fishing here during January and February. The reservoir is stocked with rainbow trout and has a population of hybrid Bass. Not a bad place to go to shrug off the winter fishing blahs.

Chickahominy Reservoir

In the 80's this was one hell of a fishery. Then the drought (and maybe some other factors) caused this reservoir to go dry. I'm sure, in time, this reservoir will return to its past quality. Keep your eyes on what's happening on this once-prolific resource.

Duncan Reservoir

This desert reservoir has had its ups and downs. If there was space, I'd tell you in depth about a call I got from Cal Jordan (one of the fine fly fishers and gentlemen I've had the privilege of fishing with) about meeting him to fish Duncan Reservoir. In short, he stated he'd had the best fly fishing he'd ever experienced in Oregon that day. So, we went the next day, and between us, we didn't have a strike. As I said, Duncan is a good fly fishery, but has its ups and downs.

Fish Lake

The lake is located on the Steens Mountain and has plenty of spunky rainbows. Fly fishing can be good from the time you can access the lake (generally late June) until late October. If you go in July, load your rig with mosquito repellent. The fall period can be beautiful and you can have the lake nearly to yourself.

Grindstone

This is a private fishery located on the Grindstone Ranch east of the town of Paulina. The ranch is in a high desert setting and is one of the best of its kind. The reservoirs on the ranch hold trophy-sized rainbows and brook trout. There are accommodations, food services and guides. For information, cost and reservations, call Kaufmann's Streamborn Fly Shop in Portland (see page 49).

Round, Square and Long Lakes

These lakes, near the Santiam Pass can be accessed by going to Round Lake on Forest Road 1210. You'll have to walk to Square and Long Lakes. You'll find rainbow, cutthroat and brook trout in these lakes. The fish are not large, but can be fun. If you want to take the family on a nice outing, this would be a good choice. There is a campground at Round Lake.

Thompson Reservoir

Like Chickahominy, Thompson has been hit hard by drought. As precipitation trends improve, this will again be a significant fishery. Keep asking what the conditions are on this reservoir.

Wickiup Reservoir

This is a large reservoir and has a good population of brown trout. Some are truly giants. Most people think of Wickiup as a hardware fishery, but if you take the time to learn the reservoir, Wickiup can produce excellent results for the fly fisher.

Notes

Notes

Area Fly Shops

WESTERN OREGON

The Caddis Fly Angling Shop
168 W. Sixth Street
Eugene, OR 97401
(503) 342-7005

The Fly Fishing Shop
P.O. Box 368
Welches, OR 97067
(503) 622-4607

Kaufmann's Streamborn
8861 S.W. Commercial
Tigard, OR 97223
(503) 639-6400

Dave McNeese's Fly Shop
346 High Street South
Salem, OR 97301
(503) 588-1768

The Scarlet Ibis
6905 N.W. Kings Blvd.
Corvallis, OR 97330
(503) 754-1544

CENTRAL OREGON

Deschutes Canyon Fly Shop
(7 N. Highway 197)
P.O. Box 334
Maupin, OR 97037
(503) 395-2565

The Fly Fisher's Place
(230 West Main Street)
P.O. Box 1179
Sisters, OR 97759
(503) 549-3474

The Patient Angler
55 N.W. Wall Street
Bend, OR 97701
(503) 389-6208

Whitney's Sporting Goods
(490 S.W. Cascade)
P.O. Box 445
Sisters, OR 97759
(503) 549-2841

The Oasis
P.O. Box 365
Maupin, OR 97037
(503) 395-2611

Hook Wine & Cheddar
P.O. Box 3502
Sunriver, OR 97707
(503) 593-1633

The Fly Box
923 S.E. 3rd. Street
Bend, OR 97702
(503) 388-3330

Prineville Sporting Goods
346 N. Deer Street
Prineville, OR 97754
(503) 447-6883

Oscar's Sporting Goods
380 S.W. 15th Street
Madras, OR 97741
(503) 475-2962

Camp Sherman Store
P.O. Box 638
Camp Sherman, OR 97730
(503) 595-6711

EASTERN OREGON

B & B Sporting Goods
Highway 20 & W. Conley
Hines, OR 97738
(503) 573-6200

Additional Informational Sources

Oregon Department of Fish and Wildlife (ODFW) Offices

Headquarters
2501 SW First Street
Portland, OR 97207
(503) 229-5400

Central
61374 Parrell Road
Bend, OR 97702
(503) 388-6363

Southeast
237 S. Hines Blvd.
P.O. Box 8 - Hines, OR 97738
(503) 573-6582

The Dalles, (503) 296-4628
Lakeview, (503) 947-2950

Prineville, (503) 447-5111
Ontario, (503) 889-6975

Madras, (503) 475-2183
Klamath Falls, (503) 883-5732

Bureau of Land Management (BLM) Offices

Oregon State Office
P.O.Box 2965
Portland, OR 97208
(503) 231-6281

Map Distribution Unit
Room 17, State Highway Bldg.
Salem, OR 97310
(503) 378-6254

Burns District
Highway 20
Hines, OR
(503) 573-5241

U.S. and Oregon Forest Service Offices

U.S. Forest Service
P.O. Box 3623
Portland, OR 97208
(503) 326-2877

Oregon State Forestry Department
2600 State Street
Salem, OR 97310
(503) 378-2504

Deschutes National Forest
(503) 388-5664

Malheur National Forest
(503) 575-1731

Ochoco National Forest
(503) 477- 6247

Oregon Department of Tourism

595 Cottage Street, N.E.
Salem, OR 97310
(503) 378-3451

References and Other Reading Material

Oregon Sport Fishing Regulations, Oregon Department of Fish and Wildlife
—available at most Oregon sporting goods stores, fly shops and O.D.F.W. offices.

Oregon Atlas and Gazeteer, Delorme Mapping
—available at most Central Oregon book stores and fly shops.

Fishing In Oregon, Casali and Diness
—available at most Central Oregon book stores and fly shops.

Fishing Central Oregon, Clain Campagna
—available at most Central Oregon book stores and fly shops.